THE ARCHITECTURE LOVER'S

PARIS

THE ARCHITECTURE LOVER'S GUIDE TO

PARIS

RUBY BOUKABOU

WHITE OWL

AN IMPRINT OF PEN & SWORD BOOKS LTD.
YORKSHIRE ~ PHILADELPHIA

First published in Great Britain in 2021 by
White Owl
An imprint of
Pen & Sword Books Ltd
Yorkshire - Philadelphia

ISBN 9781526779977

Printed and bound in India by Replika Press Pvt. Ltd.
Design: Paul Wilkinson.

Pen & Sword Books Limited incorporates the imprints
of Atlas, Archaeology, Aviation, Discovery, Family
History, Fiction, History, Maritime, Military, Military
Classics, Politics, Select, Transport, True Crime, Air
World, Frontline Publishing, Leo Cooper, Remember
When, Seaforth Publishing, The Praetorian Press,
Wharncliffe Local History, Wharncliffe Transport,
Wharncliffe True Crime and White Owl.

For a complete list of Pen & Sword titles please contact
PEN & SWORD BOOKS LIMITED
47 Church Street, Barnsley, South Yorkshire, S70 2AS,
United Kingdom
E-mail: enquiries@pen-and-sword.co.uk
Website: www.pen-and-sword.co.uk

Or
PEN AND SWORD BOOKS
1950 Lawrence Rd, Havertown, PA 19083, USA
E-mail: Uspen-and-sword@casematepublishers.com
Website: www.penandswordbooks.com

CONTENTS

FOREWORD

PARIS IS FOR LOVERS of art, music, food ... and architecture! From the park benches and street lamps to the characteristic zinc roofs and clay chimney pots; from the solid, iron Eiffel Tower to the airy, contemporary Louis Vuitton Foundation, the city is a symphony of beautiful design that has made it a chic urban wonderland and the world's most famous setting for cinematic romance.

I have enjoyed experiencing both the timeless and the evolving sides of Paris over the years as a part-time Parisian. In no other city in the world can the humble act of consuming a coffee on the pavement in the morning feel like a scintillating event of its own. A glance up from one's café crème reveals at first the details that are distinctly Parisian: the terraces, the newspaper kiosks and the straight avenues. But then you notice the organic details. The top-floor apartment with the modern glass-wall makeover. The balcony with white gardenias instead of traditional red carnations. The Vietnamese restaurant nestled between a café and a boutique. The scooter mechanic workshop adapted into the ground floor of an old office building. The slightly crooked, weather-beaten wooden window frame that looks like it was deliberately designed to offset the precision of the centuries-old masonry. The motorbikes parked haphazardly that somehow complement the visual effect, despite disrupting the traffic (hectic, but nowhere near as crazy as Rome or Cairo). The colourful splashes of street art.

There is so much to discover in this city, and this guide was written to help you appreciate the details that you might otherwise miss as you rush from a restaurant to the opera or an underground jazz club, or from a shopping spree to the Louvre or an art opening. Yes, Paris urges you to keep moving, to take in as much in as possible on the run, but it also suggests that you slow down and appreciate the details, the city's architectural accessories (after all, the thousands of

cafés aren't there for simply consuming are they?).

Before I began writing this book, I spent a few weeks walking the streets – retracing familiar boulevards, and favourite backstreets, revisiting museums and institutions, restaurants and theatrical venues, stopping to ponder monuments I'd passed but never fully contemplated. Then one afternoon after a jog in the Buttes-Chaumont park, I climbed to my favourite contemplative perch on a rock under the Temple de la Sybille rotunda (named after an oracle in Greek mythology and a priestess of Apollo), looking over the park and the silhouette of Sacré-Coeur over on the hill of Montmartre and I realised the approach I needed to take. While it is nice to just fall across fascinating historic buildings, victorious columns and contemporary constructions while exploring a city, I always feel more invigorated if I can be active in my discoveries. Instead of just looking up and admiring a neo-classical column, where could I climb up to get a better view while musing on the story behind it? Instead of just visiting another Gothic church, when could I take in the beauty of the stained-glass windows while a Baroque flute recital from the likes of Jane Rutter lifted my spirits to the heavens? And instead of elbowing my way through a throng of tourists for a panoramic view of the city, where could I ponder Paris from above with some locals, chilling to lounge music with a refreshing beverage?

So I threw myself into the task, revisiting buildings I knew and discovering many I didn't, meeting with architects, researching at the Pavillion de l'Arsinal (the Architecture and Urban Planning Centre), reading in the Pompidou Centre library, scouring the Seine-side bookshops, hanging with a bouquiniste (see page 82), visiting châteaux, taking boat trips on the waterways, scribbling notes and taking photographs on my way.

I've written many articles and guides to help travellers get the most out of Paris. However, this guide is a little different, as while there is much to say and write about things to see and do in Paris, it is the city itself that is the main star here.

For centuries people have visited Paris to absorb the

ambiance and admire the architecture. I hope that this guide can inspire and help you to do the same. Bon voyage and make sure to keep looking up!

A note for the armchair traveller

Can't get to Paris right now? It's ok! This book caters to both the physical traveller and the armchair explorer. The practical tips for those on the ground are balanced with lots of fascinating information on Paris, so you don't need to be there to plunge into the history, imagine the events that shaped the city and discover the iconic and more quirky buildings and places around Paris. It's packed with colour photos, websites to look up (many of which often interactive experiences) and you can even have fun following the walking tours virtually via Google Maps or Google Earth. *Alors, amusez-vous bien*, wherever you are!

Ruby

Olivia Rutherford

Acknowledgements

THANK YOU to everyone who helped in the researching of this book and to those who helped make the process enjoyable, including: Jan & Hacene Boukabou, Julien Thonnard, Juliette Dumartin, Damien Gires, Hydrane Lo, James Purpura, Olivier Rozé, Lila Graffin, Corinne Jamma, Atout France, Stephanie Oley, Kate Bohdanowicz, Olivia Rutherford, Amelie Thienot, Nikola Meyer, Bruno Mercier, Kester Lovelace, Elise McLeod, Fred Pawle, Paris tourism, Jonathan Wright, Heather Williams, Janet Brookes, Paul Wilkinson, Karyn Burnham and everyone at White Owl Books, Jacques Ibert and Annaba & Fino.

The arrondissements of Paris

Paris is divided into 20 administrative districts called arrondissements, which start in the centre and spiral outwards in a clock-wise direction. Their reference is indicated in the last two digits of the postal code. Thus 75001 is the 1st arrondissement, 75010 the 10th etc.

17

La Défense

Palais des Congrès

8

Arc de Triomphe

Concorde

16

Roland Garros

Tour Eiffel

Musée d'Orsay

7

Parc des Princes

Tour Montparnasse

15

Gare Montparnasse

14

Parc des Expositions

Stade de France

18 Sacré Coeur

Parc de la villette

19

Aéroport
Charles de Gaulles

Gare
du nord

Gare
de l'Est

10

ra Garnier

2

Louvre

1

3

4

20

Cimetière
Père Lachaise

République

Place
de la
Nation

11

Notre-Dame
de Paris

Bastille

5

Panthéon

12

Bercy

Gare
d'Austerlitz

13

Aéroport
d'orly

1

INTRODUCTION – THE BUILDING OF PARIS

PARIS BEGAN AS a fishing village in about 250 BC on today's Montagne Sainte-Geneviève and possibly on the Île de la Cité, one of the two islands in the Seine. The Parisii tribe survived for 200 years until the Romans arrived. Rather than surrender their buildings to the newcomers, they burned down their wooden huts, after which the building of Paris as we know it today began.

The Romans built their city, with streets arranged in a grid, on a hill in what is now the 5th arrondissement. Three of those streets remain today: rue Saint-Jacques, rue de la Cité and rue Saint-Martin.

Other buildings to survive from the Roman period include the Cluny Monastery, built in 910, which is now the Musée de Cluny (28 rue du Sommerard, 75005); an amphitheatre at the Arènes de Lutèce (49 rue Monge, 75005);

Musée de Cluny.

The amphitheatre at the Arènes de Lutèce.

Roman columns reused in the nave of Saint-Pierre de Montmartre (2 rue du Mont-Cenis, 75018); and the Pillar of the Boatmen (circa 25 BC), depicting Gaulish deities, from the Île de la Cité and now in the Musée de Cluny.

After the fall of the Roman Empire in 450, Paris, now one of Europe's most prosperous cities, fell under the influence of the Roman Catholic Church, which built bigger, more impressive and permanent churches featuring arches, rectangular spaces, large piers, thick walls and symmetry that contrasted with the elaborate décor. These buildings were designed to enthral and communicate to a largely illiterate population. Architectural wonders such as pointed arches, twin towers, ribbed vaults and rose windows arrived by various routes from fifth-century Syria onwards via crusaders, Normans, cashed up clergy and pilgrims, and these began to adorn the Paris landscape.

Paris became a commercial and religious centre. Educational institutions flourished, including colleges that later morphed into what would become one of the world's most famous and prestigious universities, La Sorbonne (see page 141). The kings of the Capetian dynasty (987–1328) built grand hunting lodges in the forest of Saint-Germain-en-Laye. These remain today as some of France's grandest châteaux and palaces.

Paris continued to thrive under Philip ll (1165–1223), with its population doubling to 50,000 during his reign. He ordered that any new buildings must align with the existing streets,

Exterior of Maison Nicolas Flamel. © Ruby Boukabou

establishing one of the city's key characteristics.

In 1407 Nicolas Flamel built a house at what is now 51 rue de Montmorency, 75003. Many people thought Flamel had discovered the secret of alchemy and could turn ordinary metals into gold, but he was also a philanthropist who helped house the poor. His house is now the oldest stone house in Paris, and has been converted into a charming restaurant.

Charles Vlll (1470–1498) and Louis Xll (1498-1515) were so impressed with the Renaissance in Italy that they lured architects, gardeners, sculptors and artists to Paris, who gradually replaced the city's Gothic conventions with elegance, proportion and classicism.

The bridge of Notre-Dame (1507–1512) was the first Renaissance structure in Paris, designed by Italian architect Giovanni Giocondo. Only its stone-pile foundations survive. The two definitive Renaissance buildings still standing today are the Hôtel Carnavalet (16 rue des Francs Bourgeois, 75003), which is

Place des Vosges.

now a museum of the history of Paris, and the glorious Lescot wing of the Louvre, designed by Pierre Lescot (see page 55).

In 1594 Henri lV (and his counsellor the Duke of Sully) embarked on a programme to revive Paris. He built the Pont Neuf ('New Bridge'), La Samaritaine water pump, canals and tree-lined highways, and protected the forests. He added the 400m-long Grande Galerie to the Louvre Palace and introduced new restrictions regarding building lines and street widths.

In 1605 Henri IV created a Renaissance masterpiece: a green square 140m wide, surrounded on all sides by terraces with identical façades, steep-pitched blue slate roofs and dormer windows. This was an new model of city planning for Europe. Place Royale, later renamed Place des Vosges, became, and still is, one of Paris' most desirable addresses. Even if you can't afford to live here, you can still lounge on the grass by the central fountain and visit the house of its most famous former resident, Victor Hugo (see page 114).

Baroque, also known as French classicism, was introduced to Paris by the Jesuits at the start of the seventeenth century, during the reign of Louis Xlll. While Protestants in Britain and elsewhere were embracing simplicity and austerity, the Catholic Church encouraged flamboyance with high, painted ceilings, ornate columns, gilded ornaments and extravagant lighting.

In 1616 Marie de Medici, Henri IV's widow and mother of Louis XIII, commissioned architect Salomon de Brosse to design the Palais du Luxembourg, a lavish French Baroque version of a Tuscan palace, at 15 rue de Vaugirard, in the 6th arrondissement. It is an essential stop on any tour of Parisian architecture, even if you can only admire it from the outside (it

The Palais de Luxembourg.

houses the senate and is not open to the public) – the gardens are big and beautiful, as is the Medici Fountain (see pages 41 and 151).

It's worth remembering, however, that large, beautiful spaces were not available to all – in the mid-seventeenth century, Voltaire wrote in his *Embellissements de Paris* about the need for public spaces for the poorer Parisians: 'We blush with shame to see the public markets, set up in narrow streets, displaying their filth, spreading infection, and causing continual disorders.... Immense neighbourhoods need public places. The centre of the city is dark, cramped, hideous, something from the time of the most shameful barbarism.'

But back to the monarchs ... few have a more distinct architectural legacy than Louis XlV, whose gloriously Baroque Palais de Versailles is still one of the most spectacular buildings in the world. Baroque blossomed under the flamboyant Louis XlV and remained the dominant style until after the reign of Louis XV in 1774, when rococo – a

Palais de Versailles.

mashing of rocaille (stone) and cocquille (shell) – emerged.

After Louis XIV's death, several rooms at Versailles were given a rococo renovation, the most famous being the Hall of Mirrors, and the style soon became *de rigueur* in Paris salons.

A neo-classical Greek and Roman

The Hall of Mirrors at Versailles.

The Panthéon.

style emerged in the eighteenth century, during which the Panthéon, one of the city's most spectacular architectural sights, was built (see page 165).

Further restrictions were made on new buildings at this time, especially regarding height. After the French Revolution in 1789, neo-classicism was used to reassert the virtue and power of the new republic. The Arc de Triomphe (see page 68), commissioned in 1806 after Napoleon's victory in the Battle of Austerlitz, is the defining example, and is now the city's architectural centrepiece.

Napoleon also introduced Egyptian influences, following his successful campaign in northern Africa in 1803. You can see examples of this at the entrance to the German ambassador's residence (78 rue de Lille, 75018) and the Fontaine du Fellah (4 rue des Sèvres, 75007). The Egyptian influence was revived in 1921 with the Louxor Cinema (17 boulevard la Magenta, 75010), which featured Egyptian motifs and mosaics by Amédée Tiberi. After almost being demolished, it was renovated and reopened in 2013.

During the period known as the

French Second Empire (1852–1870), under Napoleon III (Napoleon I's nephew), much of the Paris we know today was created. Napoleon III commissioned Georges-Eugène Haussmann to 'aerate, unify and beautify' Paris. Haussmann was a lawyer and government official, not an architect, but as a Parisian he knew the city was becoming overcrowded, foul and prone to epidemics. He was also known for his determination to get things done. Haussmann demolished around 12,000 buildings, including his own home, to create wider, tree-lined boulevards and wider pavements, which in turn accommodated

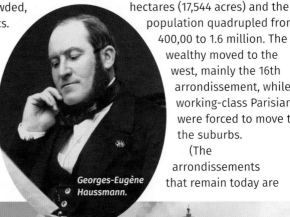

newspaper kiosks, pavement cafés and street furniture. Major intersections became grand plazas.

The next step was to divide the city into twelve arrondissements, each with its own character and trades. By 1860, the number of arrondissements had grown to twenty as the area of the city more than doubled to 7,100 hectares (17,544 acres) and the population quadrupled from 400,00 to 1.6 million. The wealthy moved to the west, mainly the 16th arrondissement, while working-class Parisians were forced to move to the suburbs.

(The arrondissements that remain today are

Georges-Eugène Haussmann.

Typical Haussmanian Building.
©Studio TTG ©Paris Tourist Board

administrative districts that start at the very heart of the city (Île de la Cité) and spiral outwards. Their reference is indicated in the last two digits of the postcode. Thus 75001 is the 1st arrondissement in the centre, (75 indicating the code for Paris), 75010 is the 10th etc.)

Haussmann and his team of architects created a unifying façade that is now the unmistakable symbol of Paris: apartment blocks made of beautiful locally-mined Lutetian limestone. The height of the new buildings was restricted to six storeys, with balconies and a mansard roof made of zinc and angled at 45 degrees to allow more sunlight for the street below, and dormer windows. The finishing touch on this is the distinctive chimney pots. Coal was expensive in the nineteenth century and a chimney pot, signifying a centrally heated home, became a symbol of wealth. These pots are ubiquitous today, but are mostly ornamental.

Haussmann's chief engineer, Eugène Belgrand, built reservoirs and aqueducts to deliver clean drinking water to the city, and 'grey' water from the canals and the Seine to wash the streets and water the gardens. Many of these pipes are still functional today. He also installed thousands of new gas street lights. The streets became safer and livelier at night, while the city became cleaner and Parisians healthier.

Haussmann hired teams of architects to build neo-classical monuments and grand railways enabling people to go on excursions to the countryside (amongst them were the Impressionist painters with their new tubes that allowed paint to be portable). The emerging middle-class built homes using Renaissance and Baroque touches to display their newfound wealth.

Haussmann cleared most of the private houses from the Île de la Cité and replaced them with administrative buildings and churches. He also commissioned Charles Garnier to design the opulent Opéra Garnier (built 1861–1875 at Place de l'Opéra, 75009). Iron was becoming widely used, replacing masonry for columns and allowing wider arches, thus making internal spaces lighter. It was used in the distinctive entrances to the Métro and for the Eiffel Tower, built in 1889, to showcase Paris' modernity.

After a huge blow-out of costs, Haussmann was forced to resign and ended his days as a pensioner in rented accommodation. But his legacy is unmistakable.

The Belle Époque (1871–1914), largely coinciding with the Art Nouveau era, was a period of optimism, wealth and relative hedonism during which the bars ('guinguettes') in Montmartre, including the famous Moulin de la Galette and the Moulin Rouge, were created.

The Art Deco period (1913–1939) introduced a style of sleek lines and

Opéra Garnier.

strong colours influenced by Modernism and Cubism. The Théâtre des Champs-Élysées (15 ave Montaigne 75008), with its reinforced concrete, symmetry, simplicity and functionality, and the Folies Bergères music hall (32 rue Richer, 75009) are prime examples. Art Nouveau and Art Deco came together in 1924 at Piscine de la Butte aux Cailles (5 place Paul Verlaine, 75013). The exterior of this swimming pool is curvaceously Nouveau while the interior has Deco-style exposed concrete arches. It is one of Paris' best-kept secrets.

Modernism dominated after the Second World War, stripping new buildings of ornamentation and, in many opinions, beauty. French character was discarded. Instead, architects were chosen from around the world and many old buildings were demolished. Critics declared 'the end of French architecture' and the dawn of the 'International Style'.

Post-war reconstruction was unstoppable, with a growing demand for housing and office space. Prefabricated mass-produced materials were used. Large numbers of identical apartment buildings, based on designs by controversial Swiss-French architect Le Corbusier (Charles-Édouard Jeanneret),

The Centre Pompidou.

were constructed close together. These projects were plain, square and dehumanising, a folly that filmmaker Jacques Tati satirises in his 1967 film, *Playtime*.

Modernism's most prominent legacy is the Pompidou Centre, named after George Pompidou, who was President of France from 1969 to 1974. It takes American architect Louis Sullivan's dictum – form follows function – to an extreme conclusion, turning the façade of the building into an overt display of undecorated purpose. It is still controversial today, although Parisians accept its presence as part of the cityscape and most architects adore it.

In 1969 the unthinkable happened. President Pompidou approved the

Tour de Montparnasse.

construction of a 209m-high monolithic office block at Montparnasse. Visible from most parts of the city, it is considered an eyesore by most, but does provide a panoramic view of the city from its public observation deck and restaurant/bar and a green redevelopment is changing the overall aesthetic.

In the mid-1970s, architects began to reject the strict rules of Modernism for fusions of styles.

German architect Martin van Trek's Les Orgues du Flandres (completed in 1980), at 24 rue Archereau, 75019, is a complex of 1,950 apartments, schools, shops and sports facilities that creates a humanist environment against a mildly brutalist backdrop. With a nod to the city's architectural heritage, the building is shaped like a church organ.

The Tour Ailllaud, by architect Emile Aillaud and completed in 1981, in western Paris, is a high-rise residential complex of connected cylinders with passageways and paved landscapes. A sense of isolation and other worldliness prevails. It too has attracted criticism for its gimmickry.

By contrast, the apartment buildings at rue des Hautes Formes in the 13th arrondissement, designed by Christian de Portzamparc in 1979, revive the graceful geometry of the Renaissance and include traditional public spaces, recreating the urban atmosphere for which Paris is best known.

When François Mitterrand became President in 1981, his aim was to restore France's reputation in the world, not on defence policy, but on buildings. He immediately acknowledged the need to revive the nation's architecture, telling his cabinet, 'There can be no policy of greatness for France without great architecture'. His most ambitious project was to renovate the Louvre, which had become to resemble an overpopulated rabbit warren. In 1989 the underground extension and glass-and-metal pyramid (designed by Chinese-American architect I.M. Pei) were opened. Parisians soon overcame their initial shock and began to love the classy renovation.

President Mitterrand also announced an international competition to design a complement to the Arc de Triomphe, on the opposite side of the Seine, which would celebrate humanitarian

La Grande Arche de la Défense.

A view through La Grande Arche de la Défense.

ideals over military victory. Danish architect Johan Otto von Spreckelsen won, and La Grande Arche de la Défense was completed in 1989, marking the bicentennial of the French Revolution.

Another project was the development of a former abattoir in the 19th arrondissement on the outskirts of Paris. Deconstructionist architect Bernard Tschumi won the competition and the park was built in 1984-1987. Unlike other entries in the competition, he did not design the park in a traditional mindset, where landscape and nature are the predominant forces behind the design. Rather, he envisioned Parc de la Villette

as a place of culture where the natural and artificial are forced together into a state of constant reconfiguration and discovery.

On 15 April 2019, Notre-Dame – the City of Light's iconic cathedral and attraction – was ravished by fire and the world stood still and watched in shock. While the 400 firefighters saved much of the cathedral and no human lives were lost (though one firefighter was severely injured), much of its 800-year plus history devastatingly went up in smoke and its spire collapsed to the gasps of the onlookers. The reaction from the French, the Catholic community and art, architecture and history lovers around the globe revealed that this was not just a building, but in fact part of the heart and soul of Paris.

'Notre-Dame is our history, our literature, part of our psyche, the place of all our great events, our epidemics, our wars, our liberations, the epicentre of our lives,' President Macron told reporters in front of Notre-Dame, as it was still on fire, promising to rebuild it together (his presidential *grand projet*?). He set a five-year time frame on the rebuilding, perhaps a little hastily as the entire structure was still under risk of collapse the following year. A debate on whether to replace the fallen spire with a replica or modern interpretation became heated. The issue was understandably delicate since the cathedral is the most famous piece of Gothic architecture in the world, with is flying buttresses, gargoyles, bell tower and rose stained-glass windows.

Today's politicians and bureaucrats have a renewed determination to maintain Paris' architectural predominance. 'A city like Paris must be able to reinvent itself at every moment in order to meet the challenges facing it,' Mayor Anne Hidalgo said in 2014. 'It is important in today's world to find new collective ways of working that will give shape to the future metropolis.' Part of this will be the residential and sporting facilities left after the 2024 Paris Olympics and an ambitious expansion of the Métro, due to be completed in 2030.

Following a series of car-free days in the first four arrondissements in 2019, Hidalgo is considering extending the practice, part of her 'Paris breathers' initiative. The initiative also includes increased planter boxes and more

Notre-Dame de Paris cathedral reconstruction site in May 2020.

bikes and electric trottinettes (stand up scooters) that became particularly handy during the 2019/2020 transport strikes. When lockdown initially ended on 11 May 2020 following the global Coronavirus pandemic, Hidalgo made the most of the occasion to ban cars from the central rue de Rivoli, with the aim to maintain some of the calmness and cleanliness that prevailed while people stayed at home.

Many other tree-covered developments are growing in and around Paris, including urban 'forests' and gardens to replace concrete squares around major monuments such as City Hall, Opéra Garnier and the Eiffel Tower. New bike lanes, outdoor climbing equipment and a gym in the middle of the Seine are also in the works, as well as revisiting unused places, such as a cocktail bar opening in a defunct Métro station (Croix Rouge in the Latin Quarter)!

The largest urbanisation project since Haussmann is being built on the Rive Gauche, the stretch of the Seine that was once known as the bohemian Left Bank. Novel façades, new buildings and thousands of trees give the impression of being in a different city or even country. By 2028 this area will house 20,000 residents and 60,000 workers.

In October 2019 the French government began a three-year project to construct a village to house 15,000 athletes in the northern Paris department of Seine-Saint-Denis in preparation for the 2024 Olympic Games. By adding 3,000 homes in the commune of Saint-Ouen and increasing the provision of sports amenities, the aim is to regenerate the suburb and address rising poverty. The plan is to emulate the legacy of London after the 2012 Olympics, which breathed new life into London's East End.

Also, in October 2019, Prime Minister Edouard Philippe announced a ten-year plan with twenty-three concrete measures in the areas of security, justice, education, healthcare and civic 'attractiveness'.

Paris has aims to become carbon neutral by 2050, meaning reducing emissions every year. With temperatures routinely rising to the 40s Centigrade (104°F) Paris must future-proof itself against heat waves. But architect Fabian Gantois stresses the importance of balance between modernising buildings and maintaining Paris' unique aesthetic. 'The Haussmann city was conceived with the idea of harmony.... We're not going to replace something seen nowhere else with something seen everywhere else,' he says. The building of Paris has emerged from the melting pots of Ancient Greece, Rome, Egypt, Assyria, Spain and Normandy through to the present day, thanks to the passions, foresight and dedication of its architects, scholars, designers, artists, sculptors, masons and rulers.

With this book you will be able to seek out the city's most charming secrets and historical delights, either in person and on foot, or through your imagination with help from the descriptions, images and links to stimulating online experiences.

AN ARCHITECTURAL TIMELINE
Identifying Architectural Styles and Periods

THE CITY OF PARIS is like a 105km² museum of architecture. From a Parisii boatman pillar, through the centuries of contrasting architectural styles, to innovative twenty-first-century projects that seek to tackle climate change, it's all laid out, asking to be discovered. There are countless museums to visit displaying relics of architectural significance in themselves, as well as hundreds of objects in the streets, places of worship, restaurants, private and public buildings and public spaces. As technologies advanced and tastes changed, buildings were altered, leading in many cases to an overlap of styles. Here are the major architectural periods to look out for, with tips on how to identify them and where to find them.

Mesolithic (c.8000 BC + Neolithic c.4500–4200 BC)

Excavations have revealed evidence of settlements in these periods, but no structures remain. There are traces of hunter/gatherer settlements, such as quarries for sharpening tools.

Features: Tools, axes, ceramics.

Where to find: Musée Carnavalet.

Parisii (250 BC–52 BC)

An ancient Celtic tribe, the Parisii settled in Montagne Sainte-Geneviève, and possibly on the Île de la Cité, one of the two islands in the Seine, and named their village Lucotocia, meaning marsh.

Features: Bridges, ceramics, axes, canoes, boatman Pillar.

Where to find: Musée Carnavalet, Musée de Cluny.

Roman (c.250 BC–c.AD 450)

Julius Caesar conquered Paris and annexed it to the Roman Empire, naming it Lutetia. As with all Roman towns, it was planned on a grid. The main axis, Cardo Maximus (now rue Saint-Jacques), runs north/south.

Features: Building materials were concrete, brick and stone. Remains include baths, arenas, columns, aqueducts.

Where to find: Musée de Cluny, the archaeological crypt under the parvis of Notre-Dame Cathedral, rue Saint-Jacques, rue Saint-Martin, Arènes de Lutèce (amphitheatre), Roman columns reused in the nave of Saint-Pierre de Montmartre.

Romanesque (c.800–1100)

Romanesque architecture was inspired by Syrian and Roman architecture, in particular semi-circular arches.

Features: Thick heavy walls, rounded arches, twin towers, decorative portals, wide aisles and dark interiors without windows, huge columns. The churches were lit by torches.

Where to find: Few examples remain, but those that do include the sculpted column in the basilica of Église Saint-Germain-des-Prés, the bell tower of Église Saint-Séverin and Saint-Pierre de Montmartre.

Gothic (c.1100–1526)

Influences from Syria and Moorish Spain saw features such as externalised structural supports (flying buttressed) introduced, which carried the buildings' weight, enabling tall arches and high interiors.

Features: Pointed arches to carry more weight, cross-ribbed vaults, flying buttresses, high ceilings, stained-glass, windows and light, gargoyles, masonry structures, gables (pitched roofs or pediments).

Where to find: Basilique Saint-Denis Musée de Cluny, Église Saint-Eustache, Église Saint-Julien-le-Pauvre, Musée Carnavalet.

Gothic Rayonnant (radiating) style (c.1200–1280)

Improving the structure enabled a decorative style with high vertical lines. Using imported materials and techniques from the Middle East, they created huge stained glass windows, resulting in a coloured light radiating from the centre.

Features: More space and light, rose windows, larger spaces, decorative motifs, tracery, fine architecture.

Where to find: The Sorbonne chapel, Église Sainte-Chapelle, Notre-Dame de Paris, Musée de Cluny, La Consiergerie.

The Renaissance (c.1515–1643)

Charles VII and Louis Xll returned from the Italian wars at end of the fifteenth century and early sixteenth century bringing architect Sebastian Selio's manual. Classical architecture returned with elegant French adaptations.

Features: Ancient classical orders (column structures) with new French orders added, perspective, circular and square shapes, growth in urban planning, *hôtels particuliers* (private mansions) with unified façades and heights built for the aristocrats on monumental geometric squares. Gothic churches began to include Renaissance architecture.

Where to find: Pont Notre-Dame foundations, Musée Carnavalet, The Lescot wing of the Louvre, Place des Vosges, Place Dauphine, Musée de Cluny, Fontaine des Innocents, interior of Église Saint-Eustache.

French Baroque and Classicism (seventeenth century)

The Roman Catholic Church introduced

this decorative and flamboyant style to inspire the masses as a counter to the simplicity and austerity adopted by the proponents of the Protestant Reformation. It blossomed under the flamboyant Louis XlV, the Sun King, giving way to neo-classicism by the end of Louis XV's reign in 1774.

Features: High-vaulted painted ceilings, ornate columns and light reflecting off gilded ornaments, oval and elliptical, solid, imposing, huge gardens. Some *hôtels particuliers* had new spaces such as dining rooms and salons.

Where to find: Palais de Versailles, Palais du Luxembourg, La Sorbonne, Hôtel de Sully, Musée Picasso, Hôtel des Invalides, Église Saint-Sulpice.

Rococo (1715–1774)

This late-Baroque style catered for the increasing growth and wealth of the middle-class with reduced influence of the monarchy. It flourished for a short period after Louis IV's death.

Features: Intricate, asymmetrical shapes, ornamental, delicate, curvilinear and colourful, introduction of wrought iron decoration.

Where to find: Prime Minister's residence Hôtel Matignon, Hôtel de Soubise, the clock room in Versailles.

Neo-classicism (1667–1830)

Inspired by ancient Greece and Rome, neo-classicism started during the reigns of Louis XIV and Louis XV. Many of these buildings remain today.

Louis XVI style (1774–1793)

Parisians abandoned the elaborate decorative rococo style and focused on ancient, grander classical themes, ordered nature and beauty. They were inspired by archeological discoveries, especially Pompeii and the 'Grand Tours' of ancient sites.

Features: Slender, elegant, Corinthian columns, lintels and architraves, symmetry and straight lines, harmony and balance.

Where to find: Palais de la Légion d'Honneur, Palais de Justice entrance gate, Théâtre de l'Odéon, Comédie Française.

Empire style (1800–1820s)

Emperor Napoleon I aligned himself and France with the grandeur of Rome and Greece and its perceived morality and standards. He identified France with the Enlightenment.

Features: Greco-Roman and Egyptian forms and motifs, straight columns, simple square designs, a new straight boulevard, uniform façades.

Where to find: Vendôme Column, Arc de Triomphe, La Madeleine, Palais de Louvre, Hôtel Biron (Musée Rodin), Panthéon, Place de la Concorde, Palais de la Bourse, rue de Rivoli and its arcades, Arc de Triomphe du Carrousel, grand stairway of the Palais de Luxembourg.

Restoration (1814–1830)

The restoration of the monarchy followed the defeat of Napoleon I in 1815. Louis XVIII and Charles X sought to restore the reputations of the monarchy and re-dedicate monuments while continuing with building programmes.

Beaux-Arts/Louis-Philippe Style (1830–c.1900)

This style challenged the conservatism of the Académie des Beaux-Arts and rigid neo-classicism and was named after the school where it was taught, the École des Beaux-Arts. It incorporated Romanesque and neo-classicism with Gothic and Renaissance elements, establishing a distinctive French style. It sought to reflect the region and the purpose for which it was built. It was embraced by the bourgeoisie (wealthy class).

Features: Sculptures, murals, artworks and mosaics reflected the essence of the building. New technologies were applied to glass and cast iron framework to create light and space. Rustication (creating a rough surface).

Where to find: Palais Garnier, Gare d'Orsay, École des Beaux-Arts, Bibliothèque Sainte-Geneviève, Grand Palais façade, Hotel de Ville, Muséum national d'histoire naturelle, Palais de Justice.

Second Empire Style/Napoleon III (1848–1870)

Napoleon III oversaw the growth of a railway network that facilitated commerce throughout France. He promoted business and export, as civic buildings, industries and other businesses continued to spring up. Existing buildings were adapted to suit their new use and new technologies were applied. As Paris became more prosperous, Napoleon III appointed the Prefect of Paris Georges-Eugène Haussmann to 'aerate, unify and beautify' the city. The Haussmann renovations took place from the 1840s to the early-twentieth century.

Features: Wide avenues, impressive square monumental buildings using classical styles, rich colouring and decoration. Apartment blocks made of stone, restricted to six storeys, with balconies and a mansard roof made of zinc and angled at 45 degrees to allow more sunlight for the street below, dormer windows and chimney pots. Parks, squares and green spaces.

Where to find: Avenue de l'Opéra, Interior of Opéra Garnier, Gare du Nord, Buttes-Chaumont, Louvre Richelieu wing, Place du Carrousel, Bois de Boulogne, Parc Monceau.

Art Nouveau (1893–1917)

The relaxing of building codes allowed for a departure from the stricter Haussmannian structures and added movement and imagination.

Features: Flowing and stylised, brightly coloured and pastels, plant and organic motifs made of glass and wrought iron.

Where to find: Entrance to Métro Abbesses, the new Bouillon Chartier, Grand Palais interior, Castel Beranger, Pont Alexandre lll lamp posts, Maxims, Galeries Lafayette, Église Saint-Jean-de-Montmartre, Printemps Haussmann, La Samaritaine.

Art Deco and the Modern Movement (1918–1939)

Influenced by Cubism and Byzantine architecture, Art Deco became popular between the First and Second World Wars.

Features: Sleek lines, strong colour schemes, modernist, reinforced concrete, ceramics, symmetry, simplicity, geometric lines, functionality, setbacks for each floor to allow for terraces.

Where to find: Théâtre des Champs-Élysées, Folies-Bergère, Louxor cinema, Le Grand Rex cinema, Palais de Chaillot, Piscine (swimming pool) Butte-aux-Cailles interior, the original Bouillon Chartier (restaurant) in the 9th arronidssement, La Samaritaine, the Eiffel Tower, Théâtre de Champs-Élysée, Palais de Chaillot, Palais de Tokyo, Tour Montparnasse, Angelina Paris (tearoom), Café de Flore, La Coupole brasserie.

Modernism (1918–1970s)

The aim of Modernism was to use improved materials to create functional and unique buildings for better living conditions but with minimalist geometric structures, functional but industrial-looking: 'form follows function'.

Post-Second World War (1945–1970s)

Following the Second World War, a massive rebuilding programme led to the expansion of the city limits, high-risers were built to replace destroyed houses to provide better, more hygienic living conditions and to meet the growing demand for office space. Many old buildings were less valued and torn down.

Features: Glass, steel, concrete, geometric, elimination of ornament, stilts, strip windows, roof terraces, in-built furniture. Identical buildings, improved housing conditions such as the inclusion of private bathrooms. French character was erased in favour of the International Style in high rises that created heavily populated districts.

Where to find: The Swiss Pavilion, Cité Internationale Universitaire, Fondation Le Corbusier, Atelier (studio) Brancusi.

Post-Modern (1970s–2000s)

Architects rejected the strict rules of Modernism, regarded it as cold and alienating. They applied both classical and computer-aided components to create eye-catching structures. Presidents Georges Pompidou and

François Mitterrand transformed and revitalised the city.

Features: Colourful, playful, daring, imaginative and surprising. Allows for local flavour with curved forms and is often asymmetric. Breaks away from the traditional shape of purpose-built structures.

Where to find: Centre Pompidou, Grand Arche de la Défense, Parc de la Vilette, La Cinematèque Française, Bibliothèque National de France, Fondation Cartier, Les Orgues du Flandres, Ricardo Bofill's Les Espaces d'Abraxas, Opéra Bastille, Le Siège du Parti communiste français (Communist Party HQ).

Deconstructivism

The breaking down of structures and playing around with form and volume to discover its possibilities. The French philosopher Jacques Derrida coined the term and his friend, architect and philosopher Peter Eisenman, developed the idea of fragmenting a building and exploring the asymmetry of geometry creating discomfort and confusion. While this sounds anti-architectural, it

can be understood in the creations.

Features: Distortion, surface manipulation, fragmentation, exposed material, large expanses of material. Computer-aided design.

Where to find: Parc de la Villette, Philharmonie de Paris, Fondation Louis Vuitton, La Cinémathèque Française.

Contemporary (from 2001)

Architecture continues to be imaginative and surprising with no particular style, but an increasing awareness of the need to live more sustainably to create a healthier living environment.

Features: Living foliage, recycled water, solar electricity and other sustainable measures. Buildings and spaces are re-purposed and material is re-used or recycled. Pedestrian and bike-friendly areas expand and more socially-friendly public housing is constructed.

Where to find: Louvre Pyramid, Fondation Louis Vuitton, Musée du quai Branly, Quartier des Halles, Cité de la Mode et du Design, Origami Office Building. Manuelle Gautrand.

36 HOURS IN PARIS

ONLY IN PARIS for a few days and overwhelmed by the options? Follow this suggested itinerary for an unforgettable trip.

Day One

Morning: Bonjour! Begin your day like a Parisian, with coffee and a croissant at a café. Either perch at the bar – the staff are a wealth of local knowledge if you can get on their good side (it's also a lot cheaper!) – or find a table on the terrace from which to scrutinise the surrounding architecture and street fashions. Then take the Métro to Arts & Métiers (Lines 3 and 11).

People relaxing under the Eiffel Tower.
Ruby Boukabou

Follow the walking tour of the Marais (see page 188) where you'll discover the oldest stone house in Paris (house of Nicolas Flamel), the Pompidou Centre (which also offers a panoramic view of Paris), seventeenth-century mansions that have been transformed into museums, Louis XIII's Saint-Paul-Saint-Louis church, and Paris' charming first planned square – Place des Vosges.

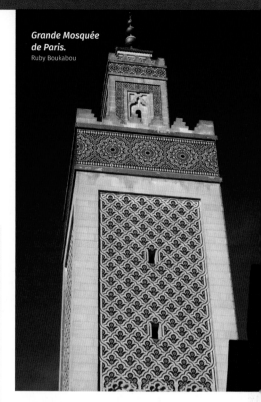

Grande Mosquée de Paris.
Ruby Boukabou

 Lunch at the famous Art Nouveau Brasserie Bofinger (5-7 rue de la Bastille, 75004 **www.bofingerparis.com**). This classic Parisian brasserie founded in 1864 boasts Belle Époque décor with an elegant use of mirrors, brass and tiles, and an exceptionally pretty floral stained-glass dome. Not only have French presidents dined here, it was once a showbiz haunt (Gene Kelly and Maurice Chevalier were two of their star clients).

Afternoon: Take the Bastille - Grande Mosque walking tour (see page 196), checking out the Bastille Opéra, the Pavillon de l'Arsenal (the architecture and urban planning centre), the banks of the Seine, the mesmerising Arab World Institute, the Seine-side sculpture gardens and the Jardin des Plantes. Enjoy a mint tea and in the neo-byzantine Grande Mosqée de Paris.

Evening: Explore Saint-Germain with an apéro at one of the oldest coffee houses in Paris, Café de Flore (172 boulevard Saint-Germain, 75006), dinner at industrial-chic Semilla (54 rue de Seine, 75006) and a night cap with old-world charm in the bar of boutique hotel, L'Hôtel (13 rue des Beaux Arts, 75006) or with the cool art crowd at La Palette (43 rue de Seine, 75006).

Day Two

Morning: Follow Part A of the Arènes de

Fontaine de Medicis Luxembourg Gardens.

Lutèce - Eglise Saint-Julien-le-Pauvre walking tour (see page 202), which will plunge you into the ancient Roman quarter of the city and the cradle of Paris, with the Saint-Etienne-du-Mont church and stunning neo-classical Panthéon (formerly a church, now mausoleum). Visit the beautiful Luxembourg gardens.

 Lunch at Treize Bakery (5 rue de Médicis, 75006).

Afternoon: Finish the walking tour that leads you to the Odeon theatre, the Sorbonne and the Musée de Cluny (with its relics of Roman baths, and gym and medieval gems). Then visit the world-famous Shakespeare and Company bookshop (37 rue de la Bûcherie, 75005),

pay homage to Notre-Dame Cathedral (see page 86) and see the Conciergerie and/or Sainte-Chapelle. Cross to the Right Bank and walk down rue de Rivoli to the Louvre. Relax in the Tuileries or enjoy a herbal infusion at Le Meurice, visit or pass by the Orangerie museum (home to Monet's Water Lilies) to the Place de la Concorde with the Luxor Obelisk, and continue up past the Grand Palais. Have coffee in the Petit Palais and saunter up the Champs-Elysées. Look across to, or climb up, the Arc de Triomphe!

Evening: See sunset from the Eiffel Tower then sip a champagne cocktail followed by dinner at Monsieur Bleu in the Palais de Tokyo (20 avenue de New York, 75116, **www.monsieurbleu. com**). Finish the day with live jazz at the legendary underground Caveau de Huchette (5 rue de la Huchette, 75005 - check their programme, **http://www.caveaudelahuchette.fr/**) or the medieval dungeon, now a bar and jazz club with many jam sessions, Caveau des Oubliettes (52 rue Galande, 75005, free entry). https://m.facebook.com/caveaudesoubliettes/

Day Three

Morning: Visit the exquisite Opéra Garnier then stroll through one of Paris' beautiful parks (Buttes-Chuamont or Parc Monceau) or, if it's hot, cool off with a swim in the Art Deco Piscine Pontoise (17 rue de Pontoise, 75005).

Lunch at the iconic brasserie Le Bouillon Chartier, 7 rue du Faubourg Montmartre, 75009). (**www.bouillon-chartier.com**

Afternoon: Stroll through the Passage des Panoramas, a nineteenth-century covered arcade, board a ride on a Canauxrama boat along the canal, under the vault of the Bastille and along the Seine, then visit bouquiniste Cyril Graffin (quai des Grands Augustins, near the corner of Pont Neuf) before winding down with a massage or hot chocolate at a Palace Hotel (Le Bristol or Le Meurice), or coffee at Le Procope, the oldest café in Paris (13 rue de l'Ancienne Comédie, 75006).

Canauxrama boat along the canal. Ruby Boukabou

Evening: Head to Montmartre for dinner at the Terrass" Hotel (**www.terrass-hotel.com**), then wander through the streets of Montmartre, under the Sacré-Coeur, and finish with a cocktail and live jazz at Lulu White, where Paris meets New Orleans (12 rue Frochot, 75009). Santé!

View from Terrass Hotel restaurant.

PARIS PANORAMAS

Start or punctuate your architectural adventures on a literal high with a panoramic view of the city from a tower, museum or rooftop bar across the city.

Tour Saint-Jacques

Square de la Tour Saint-Jacques, 75001
www.desmotsetdesarts.com/offres/
visites-guidees-paris/visite-de-la-tour-
saint-jacques

A narrow staircase takes you 54m up to the top of this tower, a remnant of the flamboyant Gothic church Saint-Jacques de la Boucherie, which was torn down in the French Revolution. Look over the gargoyles and gasp at the 360-degree open-air view of the Seine and Paris. Book in advance and remember to wear sensible shoes!

Centre Pompidou

Place Georges-Pompidou, 75004
www.centrepompidou.fr/en
www.restaurantgeorgesparis.com

From the sixth floor of the Pompidou Centre you can see the Opéra Garnier, Sacré-Coeur Basilica and the Eiffel Tower in particularly fine view.

The Arab World Institute (free)

1 rue des Fossés Saint-Bernard, 75005
www.imarabe.org

From the rooftop on the 9th floor of the IMA (Institut du Monde Arabe) you have

Gothic church Saint-Jacques de la Boucherie.

a bird's eye view of the Seine, the Île de la Cité and the back of Notre-Dame Cathedral.

The Panthéon

Place du Panthéon, 75005
www.paris-pantheon.fr

Enjoy great views of the city, especially of the surrounding Latin Quarter, from the terrace that encircles the building's famous dome, 35m above the street. April–October only.

The Eiffel Tower

Champ de Mars, 5 avenue Anatole France, 75007
www.toureiffel.paris/en

Climb to the second floor then ride the lift to the 276m-high platform. The view is stunning but there's one strange thing: there's no Eiffel Tower! Go all out and dine in the tower at 58 Tour Eiffel. **www.restaurants-toureiffel.com**

Arc de Triomphe

Place Charles de Gaulle, 75008
www.paris-arc-de-triomphe.fr

You can climb the 284 stairs or catch the lift to the mid-level and take the remaining 64 stairs to the top. Either way you'll be breathless from the view alone. This is a great spot from which to understand how Haussmann's boulevards connect the city.

Montparnasse Tower

33 avenue du Maine, 75015
www.tourmontparnasse56.com

This 210m office skyscraper is located in the once artistic hub of Montparnasse. There are two viewing levels: the 56th floor with floor-to-ceiling windows and an open-air panoramic terrace. You can

View from the Eiffel Tower.

dine at the Ciel de Paris or, from May to the end of September, be wowed by the views with some bubbles at the Champagne Bar.

Sacré-Coeur Basilica

35 rue du Chevalier-de-la-Barre, 75018
www.sacre-coeur-montmartre.com

You may have to queue, so use the time to limber up for the 300-stair climb. The reward is glorious. But if you don't want to wait, enjoy the view from street level instead and stroll around to discover stunning vistas in all directions – Montmartre is one of the highest points in Paris.

View from the Sacré-Coeur Basilica.

Parc de Buttes-Chaumont lookout (free)

1 rue Botzaris, 75019
www.paris.fr/equipements/parc-des-buttes-chaumont-1757

The hilly and lush Buttes-Chaumont park includes a lookout with a fine view of the city, especially Sacré-Coeur. Pack a picnic and enjoy the park while you're there.

Parc de Belleville (free)

rue Piat, 75020
www.paris.fr/equipements/parc-de-belleville-1777

Belleville, in Paris' north east, is on a hill and this pretty, hilly park is topped with a 30m-high terrace that offers sweeping views of the city.

BARS WITH VIEWS

Hôtel National des Arts et Métiers

243 rue Saint-Martin, 75003
www.hotelnational.paris

The rooftop bar of this boutique hotel looks over the zinc roofs and terracotta chimney pots of the surrounding terraces, making it feel both urban and intimate.

Rooftop of Hôtel National des Arts et Métiers.
Jérôme Galland

Perchoir

37 rue de la Verrerie, 75004
Place du 11-novembre 1918, 75010
14 rue Crespin-du-Gast, 75011

Perchoir has three bars offering cocktails with a view: Ménilmontant (relaxed vibe, views of Sacré-Coeur) on rue Crespin-du-Gast in the Marais (overlooking Hotel-de-Ville and the Seine) on rue de la Verrerie, and a floral summer pop-up on the roof of Gare de l'Est in Place du 11-novembre 1918!

Perruche

Printemps de l'Homme, 2 rue du Havre, 75008
http://perruche.paris/

This rooftop bar perched on top of the menswear department of Printemps (department store) is a stylish 'pool house' designed as an escape from the busy boulevards.

Terrass" Hotel

12-14 rue Joseph de Maistre, 75018
www.terrass-hotel.com

Sunset on the terrace bar on the 6th floor here is spectacular, with the city and the Eiffel Tower sparkling in the

Terrass" Hotel bar.

distance. Or book a table inside for dinner or Sunday brunch.

Hot Air Balloon

Parc André Citroën, 75015
www.ballondeparis.com

The first hot air balloon, carrying a few animals, is said to have launched from Versailles in 1783, watched by Louis XVI and Marie Antoinette. Later that year humans tried it out from the Boulogne forest and it soon became a recreational activity for the rich. Now you too can float up and over Paris.

La Grande Roue (The Ferris Wheel)

Place de la Concorde, 75008
www.lagranderoue.eu

Besides the hot air balloon experience, there is no more impressive way to see Paris. Mid-air, you can can not only see but feel the city's topography, especially the jagged rise of Montmartre. November–May.

HOTELS

Paris' hotels range from the unique and boutique to palatial. Here is a range of architecturally interesting choices for all budgets.

Maison Albar Hotel Le Pont-Neuf

23-25 rue du Pont Neuf, 75001
www.maison-albar-hotels-le-pont-neuf. com
*****

From the outside, Maison Albar has the iconic Paris touches of wrought iron on stone, softened by red geraniums in plant boxes. From the inside, the main attraction is Paris itself. Floor-to-ceiling windows and neutral décor in the rooms allow the city to enchant you from the moment you open your eyes. The restaurant Odette features walls of dramatic, curved wood, inspired by installation artists Christo's and Jeanne-Claude's 1985 wrapping of the Pont Neuf. The French cuisine is from sisters Caroline & Sophie Rostang, sixth generation restaurateurs no less!

Hôtel Jules & Jim

11 rue des Gravilliers, 75003
www.hoteljulesetjim.com
****

Hidden behind a sober, narrow entrance, this is a lovely little hotel designed by architect Michael Malapert and interior designer Natacha Froger. The lobby doubles as an art gallery, and the twenty-three simple yet refined rooms look over the rooftops of Paris or the inner courtyard, with its magnificent plant wall,

Jules and Jim courtyard.

tables and fireplace. Inside the bar it's all wooden beams and floors with an intimate old Marais workshop style.

Hôtel Vernet

25 rue Vernet, 75008
www.hotelvernet-paris.fr
*****

Heritage and contemporary design merge in the Hôtel Vernet, built in 1914 and renovated in 2014. The Haussmann-styled façade is particularly graceful and the wood and marble interiors evoke a posh past. A glorious glass ceiling by Gustave Eiffel covers the restaurant 'V'.

Hôtel Vernet.

Interior design by François Champsaur manages to be elegant, contemporary and luxurious. The ceiling frescos are particularly fun.

Generator

9-11 place du Colonel Fabien, 75010
https://staygenerator.com/hostels/paris

Hostel
On a budget? This hostel between bustling Belleville and the trendy Canal Saint-Martin offers cheap private and shared rooms. The industrial chic design references the bohemian and has fun features such as a Métro-style bistro and bookshelf wallpaper. Its Khayma rooftop bar has views of Montmartre and there is a nightclub in the basement.

Hôtel OFF

86 quai d'Austerlitz, 75013
https://offparisseine.com
****

This unique floating hotel is moored on the bank of the Seine near the Gare d'Austerlitz. The zinc roof allows it to blend into the city but inside it's modern, bright and chic. Even if you are not staying here, you can enjoy cocktails by the pool in the evening or weekend brunch.

Yooma Urban Lodge

51 quai de Grenelle, 75015
www.yooma-hotels.com/en
***

A sharp contrast to the chic Hausmannian and refined boutique hotels, Yooma Urban Lodge is loud, bold, dramatic and vibrant. Aluminium and concrete were chosen as materials to merge with the surrounding 1970s' architecture. The façade is an electric blue with black and white stripes. Each of the 106 rooms can sleep up to six people. You'll also find a cooking school, a gym, a sauna, a restaurant and a bar.

Artist studio room at the Terrass" Hôtel.

Terrass" Hôtel

12-14 rue Joseph de Maistre, 75018
www.terrass-hotel.com
****

This delightful hotel is perched high on a street corner behind the Montmartre cemetery and close to the Moulin Rouge. The hotel was originally owned by Edmond Hurand in 1911, and apart from a brief early period, it has remained in the family ever since. The terrace on

Terrass" Hôtel facade.

the seventh floor, added in the 1950s, soon became a regular haunt for artists and musicians, and today is perfect for a sunset cocktail. A modern makeover focused on comfort and aesthetics with a theatre-feel (such as lights around the mirrors like in an actor's dressing room), enlarged rooms and the renovation of the Art Nouveau entrance canopy.

PALACE HOTELS

In 2010 the Minister for Tourism created the 'Distinction Palace' rating, awarded to hotels that met 200 strict criteria. These are all above and beyond 5-star standards. You know you are going to feel like royalty.

The Ritz Paris

15 Place Vendôme, 75001
http://ritzparis.com/

The Ritz was built in 1705 as a private mansion for Louis XIV. César Ritz, who, with French chef Auguste Escoffier, invented the modern luxury

hotel, renovated the palace to become the flagship of the new Ritz hotel chain, a synonym for opulence. It opened in 1898 and famous clientele has included Ernest Hemingway, Coco Chanel, Marcel Proust and Princess Diana. Some scenes in *How to Steal a Million* (1966), starring Audrey Hepburn and Peter O'Toole, were shot here. It was thoroughly renovated in 2012–2016 by its new Egyptian owner Mohamed Al Fayed. One can now stay in a replica of Marie Antoinette's Versailles boudoir or, for slightly less, enjoy a fancy cocktail in the Bar Hemingway.

La Réserve Paris

42 avenue Gabriel, 75008
www.lareserve-paris.com/en

Built in 1854 the Haussmann-style mansion became one of Paris' plushest hotels in 2015 with the expertise of Jacques Garcia. Think marble fireplaces, plush couches, antique mirrors, Corinthian columns and oak floors. Dining options are the Restaurant le Gabriel and the Asian fusion restaurant Pagode de Cos and the spa offers deluxe treatments.

All the palace hotels are exquisite and always a good idea for a divine hot chocolate (bonjour, Le Bristol!) or an escape from the hectic Paris streets (bonsoir, Le Royal Monceau!) where you can appreciate the works of top architects and interior designers. Besides La Réserve and the Ritz, there's:

Hôtel Le Meurice

228 rue de Rivoli, 75001
www.dorchestercollection.com/en/paris/le-meurice/

Mandarin Oriental

251 rue Saint-Honoré, 75001
www.mandarinoriental.com/paris

Hôtel Le Park Hyatt Paris Vendôme

5 rue de la Paix, 75002
www.hyatt.com/en-US/hotel/france/park-hyatt-paris-vendome

Le Royal Monceau Raffles Paris

37 avenue Hoche, 75008
www.raffles.com/paris/

L'Hôtel de Crillon

10 place de la Concorde, 75008
www.rosewoodhotels.com/en/hotel-de-crillon

Hôtel Le Bristol

12 rue du Faubourg Saint-Honoré, 75008
www.oetkercollection.com/fr/hotels/le-bristol-paris

Four Seasons Hotel George V

31 avenue George V, 75008
www.fourseasons.com/paris

Shangri-La Hotel

10 avenue d'Iéna, 75116
www.shangri-la.com/en/paris/shangrila

CAFÉS, RESTAURANTS & BARS

Most Parisians have small apartments and tiny kitchens, so often prefer to dine and socialise out. Teenagers meet in cafés, couples date over dinner, families get together for Sunday lunches at bistros, business meetings happen here, friends spend entire evenings catching up at their local and it is perfectly acceptable to go to a café alone for a drink or a meal. People also write and read in cafés. Below are some establishments where you can enjoy both a refreshment and the architecture.

Price Indications € = very cheap, €€€€€= very expensive

Angelina Paris

226 rue de Rivoli, 75001
+33 (0)1 42 60 82 00
www.angelina-paris.fr/en
€€€€

You may have to wait in line with a few dozen 20-something Instagrammers, but once inside, you'll find that this 1903 Belle Époque tearoom is as sweet and luxurious as the hot chocolates and macaroons they serve.

Au Vieux Comptoir

17 rue des Lavandières Sainte-Opportune, 75001
+33 145085308
www.au-vieux-comptoir.com
€€

This cosy, corner restaurant run by husband and wife team – sommelier Annie Bourlois and chef Cyril – is a real find. Not only is the classic set up of tightly fitted wooden tables and a mirrored wall all very cute, the French cuisine is incredible (especially their beef bourguignon).

Au Rocher de Cancale

78 rue Montorgueil, 75002
+33 1 42 33 50 29
€€€

Famous in the nineteenth century for its post-theatre suppers, this brasserie is the place for oysters and champagne, snails and fresh seafood. Its classic interior is mostly timber and is decorated with portraits of jazz musicians and nineteenth-century frescoes by illustrator Paul Gavarni.

Derrière

69 rue des Gravilliers, 75003
+33 (0)1 44 61 91 95
www.derriere-resto.com
€€€€

Feel like spending the evening in a friend's place in the Marias but, well, you don't have a friend with a place in the Marais? Derrière is a French restaurant inside a house in the 3rd arrondissement, where you can dine in the garden, the lounge room and even in the bedroom. *Oh là là.*

Café Beaubourg

43 rue Saint-Merri, 75004
https://cafebeaubourg.com/en
€€€

This industrial-smart café has a red, white and black colour scheme, a mezzanine and a terrace overlooking the square underneath the Pompidou Centre. It is a good option for a rendez-vous for champagne and foie-gras. Regulars include artists, ballet dancers and theatrical agents.

The Tour d'Argent

17 quai de la Tournelle, 75005
+33 (0)1 43 54 23 31
https://tourdargent.com/en
€€€€€

The Tour d'Argent opened in 1582 as a restaurant for noblemen and it was here that the fork made its debut in France! King Henri IV would visit to taste the famous heron pâté and it continued to be a refined address over the centuries,

with renovations making it not only a place to savour perfectly cooked duck, but also terrific Paris views.

Café de Flore

172 boulevard Saint-Germain, 75006
+33 (0)1 45 48 55 26
https://cafedeflore.fr
€€€

Arguably Paris' most famous café, Café de Flore in Saint-Germain-des-Prés was once haunt to Picasso, Ionesco, Satre, Camus, de Beauvoir and other artists and writers. The chic Art Deco interiors with mirrored walls and red seats may even inspire you to whip out a notepad or have an existential moment.

Les Ombres

27 quai Branly, 75007
www.lesombres-restaurant.com
€€€€

Les Ombres is perched on the roof of the Musée de quai Branly complex and offers fine contemporary French dining. A Jean Nouvel design (as is the museum), it is covered by a glass roof and the large terrace allows al fresco dining with the looming Eiffel Tower as the main attraction.

Buddha Bar

8-12 rue Boissy d'Anglas, 75008
+33 (0)1 53 05 90 00
www.buddhabar.com
€€€€

This is the original Buddha Bar from French-Romanian restaurateur Raymond

Visan and interior designer/DJ Claude Challe. Asian class meets French glamour in the restaurant with velvety booths, high ceilings and a huge statue of Buddha. A lush, moody upstairs bar plays the Challe's world-famous chill-out lounge music mixes.

Café A

Maison de l'Architecture
148 rue du Faubourg Saint-Martin, 75010
+33 (0) 7 71 61 10 38
www.cafea.fr
€€

Café A is an oasis in the midst of the busy, gritty Gare de L'Est hub. It is located inside the old Récollets Convent and has a refurbished casual/chic interior and a pretty garden terrace with a relaxed vibe. The building also houses the Maison de l'Architecture so you're likely to bump shoulders with some of the city's talented and up and coming architects and researchers over your organic wine and cheese platter.

Comptoir Général

80 quai de Jemmapes, 75010
+33(0) 1 44 88 24 48
www.lecomptoirgeneral.com
€€€

An evening at the Comptoire Général feels like you're at a party at someone's rich eccentric uncle's house. It has black and white checked floors, high ceilings with wooden beams, plants (including a jungle area for smokers) and decorations of African art, books and artefacts. The entrance is discreet, set back off the street by the Canal

Café A.

Comptoir Général.

Belleville Métro with a dramatic Chinese entrance and red carpeted staircase that fans up to a large central restaurant with dozens of round tables and kitsch Chinese décor.

Picotin

35 rue Sibuet, 75012
+33 1 75 57 72 02
http://restaurant-picotin.fr
€€

This French restaurant with colourful walls, comfortable banquettes, wooden tables, lampshades and red curtains is a good choice for those wanting to try hearty French, home-cooked food. Comforting touches include small vases with bright seasonal flowers on the tables.

La Felicità

5 Parvis Alan Turing, 75013
www.lafelicita.fr
€€€

This 4,500m² Italian themed food hall in the 13th arrondissement, with a 1000m² terrace, has been all the rage since it opened in 2018 by the Big Mamma group. It's located by la Station F, the start-ups incubator, and serves as a sort of canteen for those working there, while also being a hit for the general public. Industrial meets cosy and inventive with cement and glass as materials and decorations including Italian themed street-art frescos, large back-lit balloons, hanging lightbulbs,

Saint-Martin (though there's often a queue and security). Once you're in, via a red carpeted corridor lit with chandeliers, you'll find the vibe is cool and fun. There's a room with African food stands, several cocktail bars are spread throughout the other rooms and there are even places to curl up with an African history book. But before long, you'll gravitate towards the dance floor. Check their site for a programme of art, film and theatrical events.

Le Président

120 rue du Faubourg du Temple, 75011
+33 (0)1 47 00 17 18
lepresident-paris.fr
€€

Step out of Paris and into China. Le Président is an institution by the

La Felicità.

rugs, tables, floral arrangements, plants, all sorts of seating and two SNCF train carriages. Order wood-fired pizza, fresh panini, hand-made pastas with 100 per cent Italian ingredients (you can choose to order via an app to save waiting in line). Top it off with a cocktail or a Tiramisu. Payment is purely by card.

La Coupole

102 boulevard du Montparnasse, 75014
+33 (0)1 43 20 14 20
www.lacoupole-paris.com/en
€€€

This famous Art Deco brasserie has pillars adorned with Impressionist portraits, an intricate geometric floor and a semi-circle of banquettes around a dramatic bronze sculpture of two people arching into a circle under a beautiful central dome. Former regulars include Man Ray, Matisse, Picasso, Josephine Baker, Mistinguett, Camus, Sartre, Gainsbourg and Birkin.

Restaurant Le Ciel de Paris

Tour Maine Montparnasse
56 ème étage
33 avenue du Maine, 75015
www.cieldeparis.com
€€€€€

The contemporary interiors with caramel colours and sculpted, organic forms at the Ciel de Paris restaurant are the design of Noé Duchaufour-Lawrance. Being 210 metres high inside the Tour de Montparnasse, the highlight, of course, is Paris itself.

Monsieur Bleu

20 avenue de New York, 75116
+33 (0)1 47 20 90 47
https://monsieurbleu.com
€€€

This restaurant and bar, inside the trendy art venue the Palais de Tokyo, is a chic address to have up one's sleeve – it's also very reasonably priced for the high standard of food and beverages. Architect Joesph Dirand was inspired by both Art Deco glamour (velvet banquets, marble/oak floors) and slick contemporary minimalism with a grey and green colour scheme. Book a table for dinner or perk up with a champagne cocktail.

Le Paris 17

41 rue Guersant, 75017
+33 (0) 145747527
www.restaurant-paris17.fr/en
€€

This traditional French restaurant with a reputation of great service and food is particularly lovely with its hanging lamps, wooden tables and patterned tiled floors. Old French advertising posters and Pernod 51 bottles serve as decorations.

Brasserie Barbès

2 boulevard Barbès, 75018
+33 (0)1 42 64 52 23
€€€

At this chic bistro opposite the Barbès Rochechouart Métro station, you can cool down with a drink in their leafy upstairs atrium, warm up with a café crème by the fireplace, or appease your appetite with their tasty French fare in the restaurant. Whatever the season, it's an oasis away from the colourful but gritty Barbès streets. Gaze through the large arched windows over the above-ground Métro from the first floor restaurant for a particularly urban view.

Brasserie Barbès. Julie Ansiau

La Rotonde Stalingrad.

La Rotonde Stalingrad

6-8 Place de la Bataille de Stalingrad, 75019

www.larotondestalingrad.com

Drink coffee, munch on pizza, see some art or go clubbing inside this beautiful neo-classical rotunda, originally designed by Claude-Nicolas Ledoux in the late eighteenth century as a toll station (see page 72).

Aux Folies, Belleville

8 rue de Belleville, 75020

www.aux-folies-belleville.fr

Folies is a Belleville institution. Once the bar of a popular cabaret (Belleville-born Edith Piaf sang here) and cinema, Folies is now one of the most popular cafés in the quartier, between the Métro and the famous street art laneway – rue Dénoyer. From 7am you'll find people dunking croissants in their coffees or munching baguettes with butter and jam and sipping black coffee while reading the paper or chatting to the friendly Kabyle staff. Then the day is spotted with people enjoying coffees, mint teas and Perriers (they don't serve food, but you're welcome to eat your Vietnamese sandwich from down the street while consuming a beverage) and at night the coffee machine is turned off, the neon sign lights up and the terrace becomes crowded with friends catching up over beer, Pastis and wine (until 2am). Mosaic tables, large windows, mirrors, and 'Folies' maps of the world decorating the bar contribute to the establishment's unique personality.

SHOPPING – DEPARTMENT STORES, LES HALLES & FASHION BOUTIQUES

An exciting new way to shop was invented in the nineteenth century with the introduction of the department store – *les grands magasins*. These followed the success of the covered passages (see page 206) where the growing affluent middle class could shop, drink coffee, and read (for a price) under protective glass ceilings and away from the filth of the pavements.

The graceful, state-of-the-art buildings offered spaces where people could buy all sorts of goods and socialise under one roof. They had natural lighting, filtered through the ornamental glass canopies and large windows, until a whole new dimension was added with the invention of electric lighting. This became an attraction in itself, although it was only embraced after people had been assured that the bright artificial lights wouldn't make them blind!

Today, *les grands magasins* are architecturally iconic and people flock to them to admire the floral Art Nouveau and chic Art Deco features (stained-glass ceilings, airy atriums, cupolas, sculptures, mosaics and gilding) as much as for the Hermès scarves and Louis Vuitton handbags. From November each year, the stores are decorated with spectacular and cheery lighting, Christmas trees and window displays.

Le Bon Marché

24 rue de Sèvres, 75007
Monday-Saturday 10am – 8pm
Thursday 10am – 8.45pm
Sunday 11am – 7.45pm

The original Paris department store was founded in 1838 and revamped completely in 1852 by Aristide Boucicaut and his wife Marguerite. Original creations, limited editions and ready-to-wear garments were displayed alongside furniture collections and cultural exhibitions (and the tradition continues today). This all new multi-purpose store boasted a coloured glass canopy, Baroque staircases, airy atrium and iron framing which set the trend with the stores that followed. The architects? Louis-Charles Boileau and the Gustave Eiffel Company. Fixed prices and sales are said to have been invented here, a reading room was introduced for husbands while their wives shopped, and rooms for the single female employees were created on the upper floors.

Over subsequent years, the Boucicauts launched a range of cultural activities for children, and opened an art gallery for under-represented artists. In 1984 the LVMH Group acquired the store. It has expanded and undergone many improvements, while respecting the original design.

Printemps Haussmann

64 boulevard Haussmann, 75009
Monday – Saturday 9.35am – 8pm
Thursday until 8.45pm
Sunday from 11am – 7pm

This 'Cathedral of Commerce' was created in 1865 by Jules Jaluzot and his wife Augustine, who cleverly positioned the store close to the Madeleine church and the Gare Saint-Lazare, the train station that linked Paris to affluent Normandy. They weren't mistaken in their choice and today over 80 million people pass by every year, many drawn in by the window displays, lights, products and air conditioning (it's warmer than many people's apartments in winter!).

The building is stabilised by a giant iron frame and clad in stone, with statues representing the four seasons welcoming shoppers. Printemps is French for spring and the major motifs in the building are flowers, baskets and plants. A giant staircase and balconies once provided an opera-like atmosphere where shoppers would go not just to purchase goods, but to see and be seen; it was eventually removed to create more commercial space. A contemporary vertical atrium, however, allows one to glimpse the various levels. Treat yourself to a hot chocolate in the Art Deco-styled brasserie under the magnificent stained-glass dome by René Binet, with twenty-one shades of blue pink, gold and green. Or if it's a

Ruby Boukabou

Ruby Boukabou

pleasant day, there's Peruche, the rooftop bar (modelled on a pool house), on the 9th floor of Printemps Homme (the men's department) where you can sip a cocktail and gaze over the capital.

Galeries Lafayette Paris Haussmann

40 boulevard Haussmann, 75009
Monday-Saturday 9.30am – 8.30pm
Sunday 11am – 8pm
Gourmet: Monday – Saturday 8.30am – 9.30pm, Sunday 11am – 8pm

Just across from Printemps is Galeries Lafayette Paris Haussmann, opened in 1895 by Alsatian cousins, Alphonse Khan and Théophile Bader. The cousins became instantly successful when they made small adjustments to haute couture designs that they observed at prominent events and made their own more affordable ready-to-wear labels. The outside of the building is typically Haussmannian, although 1932 alterations by Pierre Patout on the rue de la Chausée-d'Antin entrance are Art Deco-styled with intricate terracotta cladding.

The interior is breathtaking – five levels of stands looking across at each other over gilded wrought iron balconies

Boukabou

with the pièce de résistance being a mesmerising 43m-high atrium roof with floral Art Nouveau/Baroque-styled designs, by Édouard Schneck. Chestnut leaf reliefs on the walls symbolise prosperity (which is what you need to shop here). In 1951 Galeries Lafayette built the highest escalator in Europe. Take it to the top floor for a view over the back of Opéra Garnier and Paris.

Rooftop Galeries Lafayette. Ruby Boukabou

During winter there's usually a mini ice-skating rink for the kids.

La Samaritaine

19 rue de la Monnaie, 75001

Founded in 1870 by Ernest Cognacq and developed with his wife Marie-Louise Jaÿ, who brought her savoir-faire from the Bon Marché, La Samaritaine was a major player of the *grands magasins*.

Architects Frantz Jourdain and Henri Sauvage chose to work with iron, glass, wood and copper and installed a modern visible steel frame with ceramic panels that advertised what was on offer, including state of the art lighting and heating, clothing, décor, furniture and more. A relief of Christ and the woman of Samaria at Jacob's well, as recounted in the Bible, also marked the façade. The interior highlights were the iron and glass canopy, ornamental balustrades and glass and brick floors, allowing natural lighting.

More Art Nouveau elements were introduced in 1912 and included mosaics and motifs of trees, flowers, grapes and peacocks. When the Art Nouveau trend waned, Henri Sauvage created a new Art Deco additional feel, which favoured more simple geometric shapes.

The UNESCO listed monument has had a major renovation by the LVHM group and has been transformed into a swish complex with a department store, a 5-star Palace hotel, restaurants, offices, a crèche and social housing, merging contemporary design with heritage elements. It reopened in 2021.

Ruby Boukabou

Le BHV Marais

52 rue de Rivoli, 75004
Monday – Friday 9:30am – 8pm
Saturday 9:30am – 8:30pm
Sunday 11am – 8pm

The Bazar de l'Hôtel de Ville is a popular department store in the Marais and has run under the Lafayette banner since 1991. The store was originally opened by a street vendor called Xavier Ruel who, shortly after moving to Paris in 1852, realised that this was the most lucrative location in the city and so decided to set up a permanent shop. Over the years he and his wife purchased more space, and more levels. When he died in 1900, the business was booming. Renovations took place and in 1913 a rotunda by architect Auguste Roy was constructed. At night, head to the rooftop bar Perchoir to enjoy a fantastic view over the Hôtel de Ville and the Seine.

Les Halles

Monday – Saturday 10am – 8:30pm
Sunday 11am – 7pm

Referred to by novelist Émile Zola as the 'belly of Paris', this central food market was commissioned to architect Victor Baltard by Baron Haussmann. Constructions began in 1851. Twelve prefabricated pavilions, with foundations in brick, used glass and cast iron for the massive halls. In 1969 the pavilions were torn down and in 1979 a new shopping centre was built, the Forum des Halles, which sits over the RER and Métro. Inside it's a rabbit warren of stores with all the usual suspects – H&M, Sephora, Zara, FNAC etc.

Architects Patrick Berger and Jacques Anziutti won the competition for a reconstruction with their major feature: a curved glass roof canopy made of 18,000 pieces of glass, supported by 7,000 tonnes of steel with the aim to create a sense of fluidity and to diffuse a soft light through the centre in all weather. Opened in 2018 it has been criticised as looking like an airport – other more inventive propositions included rooftop gardens and a lake. A large public garden has been introduced near the main entrance and a cultural centre is now also housed within, including a media centre and music conservatory.

Shopping in Pretty Places

The Marais (75003/75004)

The Marais (see page 188) is famous for its chic fashion boutiques snuggled alongside one another on narrow streets. Enjoy a shopping spree on rue de Francs Bourgeois (Uniqlo, Muji, Repetto, Ted Baker...), gazing up to the stately seventeenth-century private mansions (*hôtels particuliers*) with their symmetrical rectangular windows, columns and manicured courtyard gardens, many of which are now museums. Duck down the charming cobblestoned rue des Rosiers (Minelli, Adidas, Héroïnes, IKKS...), famous for its falafel joints. And don't miss Merci (111 boulevard Beaumarchais), a spacious and chic concept store in a renovated nineteenth-century fabric factory that sells homeware, clothes, stationery and furniture. It also has a delightful bookshop/café donating some of its profits to charity.

Triangle D'Or (75008)

Be wowed by the flashy flagship haute couture stores while prancing around the fancy 8th arrondissement. The Triangle D'Or (golden triangle) refers to the area between the avenue Champs-Élysées, avenue Montaigne and avenue George V. Think Chanel, Dior, Yves Saint Laurent, Hermès. The stores are on the street level and first floors of classic Haussmannian buildings, and flaunt their wares in large windows. The interiors are elegant and spacious with high ceilings and dramatic features such as spiral staircases.

Rue St Honoré district (75001)

Designer boutiques, concept stores, perfumeries and major fashion brands are huddled along this narrow central Parisian street on the ground floors of chic Haussmannian styled buildings. (Hugo Boss, Hublot, The Kooples, Sandro, Emporio Armani …). Then stroll through the neo-classical Greco-Roman arcades of the parallel rue de Rivoli, designed by the dynamic duo Charles Percier and Pierre Fontaine, whose other designs include the monumental Arc de Triomphe du Carrousel just across the road in the Tuileries (see page 68).

3

TRAIN STATIONS – 'GARES'

Gare d'Austerlitz Clock. Ruby Boukabou

THE INTRODUCTION OF the French rail system was originally blocked by a conflict of political interests and transport companies who used the roads, canals and rivers. After the turbulence of the Napoleonic Wars, however, Napoleon lll was intent on improving public infrastructure and morale. A large number of the middle classes were able to invest and the emperor managed to combine public and private interests, reaching a consensus in 1842.

The opening of the railways was an exciting time for Parisians as it enabled those who could afford the tickets to take day trips or weekend excursions. This was especially welcomed by the Impressionist artists, who took off to the countryside with their newly-invented easels and paint tubes.

While remaining both landmarks and the doorways to many national and international destinations, the train stations in Paris also connect local transport and create urban hubs. When travelling through them, raise your eyes from your maps to consider the architecture.

Gare Saint-Lazare

13 rue d'Amsterdam, 75008

The Gare Saint-Lazare was inaugurated in 1837, and rebuilt in 1841–1843 just to the south of its original location. In 1853, iron and glass train sheds were added

Gare Saint-Lazare, *Claude Monet, 1877*

'l'heure de tous.
Ruby Boukabou

featuring groundbreaking iron lamination techniques that allowed 40m spans without intermediary support. These were evocatively depicted by the Impressionist artist Monet in his 1877 'Gare Saint-Lazare' series, revealing his fascination with light and steam. In 1887, a hotel and five new train sheds were added for the 1889 Universal Exhibition. The imposing glass and iron roof allowed a modern feel with lots of natural light.

A century later, in 1985, President Mitterrand commissioned two works by the American/French sculptor Arman – 'consigne de vie', a tower of suitcases in the Cour de Rome, and 'l'heure de tous' in the Cour du Havre, a tower of old clocks displaying various times, stuck together; a poetic touch for the porthole of international destinations and time zones.

A shopping centre was introduced in 2012 to serve commuters, joining three levels (street, trains and Métro) while respecting the original architecture, using stone (referencing the nineteenth century), light granite floors, wood and glass (protective and transparent) and metal (historically modern).

Discover the station at the beginning of walking tour # 6 (see page 213).

Gare de l'Est

Place du 11-novembre 1918, 75010

The Gare de l'Est opened in 1849 and became a model for various other stations with its iron frame, arches and light-filled hall. A figure of a man representing Strasbourg stands proudly on top of the central axis and the names of cities in the east of France are displayed on plates on the façade. As the name indicates, trains arrive here from the east of France and Europe, as well as from the suburbs. It's a short walk to the Canal Saint Martin where you can lounge by the banks or hang out in the trendy bars and restaurants.

Gare du Nord

18 rue de Dunkerque, Paris, 75010

Close by Gare de l'Est is the Gare du Nord, which in its turn links the northern suburbs, and national and international cities such as Lille, Brussels and Amsterdam, as well as offering the Eurostar service to London. The grand neo-classical façade is topped with twenty-three statues of women representing northern France and European cities, crafted by prominent sculptors of the day. The interior of the 38m-high hall is supported by cast iron pillars. French superstar designer Philippe Starck has reinvented the Eurostar business class lounge in the style of a plush Parisian apartment.

A 2019 €600m renovation plan (in the lead up to the 2024 Olympics) to create shops, walkways, split-levels and escalators in a huge glass structure became controversial and opposed by architects, including Jean Nouvel, claiming it would deform the elegant, historic building.

Gare de Lyon

Place Louis-Armand, 75571
This massive iron railway hall has a glorious street façade with a 67m-high clock tower that helps you relax (or panic!) if approaching in traffic for your TGV for the French Riviera. An original station was built in 1855 but burnt down in 1871 during the Paris Commune. The elaborate new stone building was redesigned for the 1900 World Fair, although not completed until 1902.

The tracks lead from behind the station to destinations such as Marseilles, Cannes, Nice, and further abroad to Switzerland, Spain and Italy. There are two main halls and an underground for the Métro and for trains to the suburbs. Inside you'll find your

usual bakeries, news agencies and ticket desks and machines. The pearl of the station, however, is the neo-baroque brasserie Le Train Bleu.

Gare d'Orsay (now Musée d'Orsay)

1 rue de la Légion d'Honneur, 75007

This neo-baroque masterpiece on the Left Bank of the Seine was built for the World Fair of 1900, to be close to the Grand Palais exhibition space. It also housed a hotel (practical for the days of suitcases without wheels!). When Montparnasse train station was built and took over the railway traffic, President Giscard d'Estaing initiated a transformation of the station into a nineteenth-century art gallery. The Musée d'Orsay is one of the most popular Paris museums today, with hundreds of

Gare de Lyon station. Ruby Boukabou

The Musée d'Orsay (formerly the Gare d'Orsay).

Impressionism and post-Impressionism works hung in the old railway halls. After a visit, sit by the banks of the Seine and muse.

Gare d'Austerlitz

85 quai d'Austerlitz, 75013

Gare d'Austerlitz was inaugurated in 1838 as Gare d'Orléans and has had various extensions over the years. It services the centre of France among other destinations. In 1906 a viaduct crossing the Seine and an elevated platform added the Line 5 Métro, while in 1910 the station was flooded and temporarily closed. In 1997, its Belle Époque façades and roofing are some of the architectural elements that led to the station being listed as a historical monument. While in the area, discover the City of Fashion and Design (see page 121), then walk along the banks to the Bercy Park to visit Franck Gehry's unique Cinématèque Française (see page 121).

Gare Montparnasse

17 boulevard de Vaugirard, 75015

Originally known as the Gare de l'Ouest (The Western Train Station), Montparnasse was built in the 1840s and made the international news on 22 October 1895 when a steam train derailed and crashed through the station wall, plummeting 10m onto the Place de Rennes, killing one woman and injuring several passengers.

Hitler's military governor of Paris, General von Choltitz, surrendered his garrison here on 25 August 1944.

A newer station integrating offices was built during the 1960s, but torn down for the controversial high-rise tower of Montparnasse, and the current concrete station was built, then extended in 1990 to accommodate the TGV. This is where you can leave for Brittany and Normandy and take the cheaper high-speed train service, OUIGO, to Bordeaux in just over two hours (to be safe, arrive at least half an hour in advance to avoid the stress of rushing with luggage through very long, crowded corridors!).

COLUMNS, ARCHES & ROTUNDAS

MANY FREE-STANDING monuments enhance the city's classic character and are worth scrutiny from up close. Some you can climb to access panoramic views, some you can picnic by or jog around and others you can enter for coffee, pizza, wine … or even a boogie.

Column in Place de Chatelet, above the Fountain du Palmier.
Ruby Boukabou

COLUMNS

Fontaine du Palmier (1808)

Place du Châtelet, 75001

This 1808 Roman-styled column above Napoleon's victorious fountain in the Place du Châtelet is named after the sculpted palm leaves at the top. It commemorates Napoleon's victorious Egyptian campaign. The original gilded bronze Victory angel at the top by sculpture Louis-Simon Boizot is now in the Carnavalet Museum, but the faithful copy still has a mesmerising effect. Gaze up and around at the four statues representing Vigilance, Justice, Strength and Prudence, and at the fountain's sphinxes.

Colonne de Medici (1575)

Bourse de commerce (Stock market)
2 rue de Viarmes, 75001

Inspired by the Renaissance-styled Trajan's Column in Rome, this 31m

Colonne de Juillet.
Ruby Boukabou

column was built by Jean Bullant for Catherine de' Medici's astrologer Cosimo Ruggieri to climb the 147 internal steps to foresee the future in the sky. The former glass viewing platform is now an iron frame and no, it's unfortunately not accessible for the stargazers among us. The column is all that remains of de' Medici's manor house, the former Hôtel de Soissons.

Colonne de Juillet (1840)

Place de la Bastille, 75011

This 47m-high and 4000kg Corinthian-style column, standing on the site of the former Bastille prison, commemorates the 1830 Revolution that saw the fall of King Charles X and the start of the July Monarchy of King Louis-Philippe. The monument was constructed by architect Joseph-Louis Duc in 1840 with a base of white marble and bronze bas-reliefs including a lion and some roosters. The names of the fallen of the 1830 Revolution are engraved in gold on the sides. On the top is a gilded globe and a bronze statue by Augustin Dumont: the Génie de la Liberté (Spirit of Freedom), poised on one leg and sporting wings and a star on his head. He is holding broken chains in one hand and the flame of humanity in the other. When the sun is out, it's both a magical vision and a handy landmark. You'll discover it on the Bastille – Grande Mosquée walking tour (see page 196).

Colonne Vendôme.

Colonne Vendôme

Place Vendôme, 75001

A procession of the mighty have proclaimed their prowess from the centre of Place Vendôme. A statue of Louis XlV on horseback watched over the square from 1699 to 1792. Next, the figure of Napoleon I in Roman dress stood on a column built in 1810 to commemorate the Battle of Austerlitz and finally, in 1833, Napoleon the Emperor, in his iconic garb, rose again! The 44.3m high column is made from stone, covered by bronze from cannons seized from the Russian and Austrian armies. Classically -styled bas-reliefs decorate the column with battle scenes and representations of medals. The intricate details, the impressive height and vivid aquatic jade colour combine for a mesmerising effect.

Obélisque de Louxor

Place de la Concorde, 75008

Muhammad Ali Pasha, ruler of Ottoman Egypt, offered this ancient obelisk from Luxor to the French in exchange for a mechanical clock. The Egyptians got the bad end of the deal though, because the clock broke during shipping. The obelisk, a 23m gold-tipped granite column from Ramses II's temple, was erected in 1836 in the Place de la Concorde. The hieroglyphics site a hymn to the sun – much needed during the colder, greyer months in northern France! (see also page 160)

Obélisque de Louxor.

Les Colonnes de la Barrière du Trône

Place de la Nation, 75011

These two 28m neo-classical columns in Place de la Nation are remnants of a 24km (15 mile) farmers' tax wall barrier around Paris, erected secretly and hastily in 1787, which tripled the size of the city.

On 12 July 1789, an outraged mob of already heavily-burdened workers climbed the wall and burnt the toll houses. The use of the wall was re-imposed briefly in 1790 and again in 1798. The columns were decorated with allegorical figures and in 1845 Louis-Philippe had the statues of Saint Louis and Philip Augustus mounted on top.

Les Colonnes de la Barrière du Trône.

ARCHES
Arc de Triomphe du Carrousel
Place du Carrousel, 75001

This neo-classical monument, with one large arch between two smaller arches, was built by the influential architect/interior designer duo Charles Percier and Pierre Fontaine between 1806 and 1808, inspired by the Constantine Arch in Rome. Its purpose was to mark Napoleon's victory at Austerlitz and to serve as a grand entrance to the Tuileries Palace.

Bas-reliefs of key victories during the the campaign decorate the monument, eight Corinthium-styled columns in red and white marble are each topped by a statue of a soldier of the Grand Army and on the very top is a chariot, pulled by four horses. The original crowning was in bronze taken from the Basilica in Venice, but in 1815 these were returned and replaced by copies.

It's a particularly moving experience to walk under its arches when a young virtuoso violinist is playing something like Pachelbel´s Canon and pink bubbles from another busker float through....

Arc de Triomphe de l'Étoile
Place Charles de Gaulle, 75008
www.paris-arc-de-triomphe.fr/en

Napoleon's enormous and iconic Arc de Triomphe de l'Étoile was commissioned to Jean-François Chalgrin with an aim to glorify the emperor's victories. It was opened by King Louis-Philippe in 1836. Situated at the top of the Champs-Elysées, on the highest point of western Paris, it is the centre of the historic axis. Twelve grand avenues shoot off around it like a star (étoile).

The arch was in part inspired by the Arch of Titus in the Roman Forum, constructed in the first century, but while this was 50ft high (15.24m), Napoleon's rises to 164ft (50m)!

High-relief sculptures celebrating military victories feature on the four pedestals. La Marseillaise (officially called 'The Departure of the Volunteers of 1792') is the most famous and was designed by the sculptor François Rude, representing the original French citizen army of 1792. A female warrior with wings, dressed in classical armour, lunges dramatically as young and old men clamber forth with swords and shields. You may recognise the scene – it's another take on 'Liberty Leading the People' by Romantic painter Eugène Delacroix that hangs in the Louvre.

Other details to look out for include the carved roses in the barrel vault of the arch, hundreds of names of generals and battles, and the Tomb of the Unknown Soldier (under the arch since 1921).

Today the arch serves to represent all French victories while commemorating the sacrifices of French soldiers.

Climb up 284 steps (or take an elevator part of the way) to reach the observation deck on the top. Tickets and access on website.

Arc de Triomphe de l'Étoile.

Grande Arche de la Défense

1 Parvis de la Défense, 92800
www.lagrandearche.fr/en
Rooftop promenade 10am – 7pm (Last Admission 6.30pm)

As part of President Mitterrand's *Grands Projets*, this arch was constructed in La Défence – the business district just out of central Paris. Danish architect Johan Otto von Spreckelsen won the design competition and his work was completed by French architect Paul Andreu and Danish engineer Erik Reitzel, adding a 'cloud' – fibreglass canopies to protect against the elements. The 110m-high arch/cube has twelve pillars and a pre-stressed concrete frame covered in Carrara marble. It was inaugurated in 1989 for the bicentenary of the French Revolution and serves as a monument to humanitarian ideals. Both sides house government offices. The arch ends the historical axis that starts with the Louvre and passes through the Arc de Triomphe. It forms a secondary axis with the Montparnasse Tower and the Eiffel Tower. Le Nôtre would be impressed!

In 2017 Eiffage Constructions (in partnership with Velode and Pistre architects) completed a twenty-seven-month renovation. Glass and granite replaced the original Carrara marble. The 115m^2 floor surface was covered with glazed marble. Climb the stairs for a view, or better still, take the panoramic elevator to the rooftop promenade for breathtaking views (ticketed).

Porte Saint-Denis

Boulevard St Denis, 75010

Inspired by Rome's Titus Arch and Trajan's Column, the Porte Saint-Denis was the first of Paris' triumphal arches, serving as the doorway to Paris for the kings returning from victories in the north. It was built in 1672 for Louis XIV and features Egyptian motifs and a base with Latin inscription of Louis' victories, with two miserable figures representing the Rhine and the Dutch Republic (to really rub it in!). Just 200m down the boulevard is Porte Saint-Martin.

Porte Saint-Denis. Ruby Boukabou

Porte Saint-Denis detail. Ruby Boukabou

Porte Saint-Martin

Boulevard St Denis, 75010

Built in 1674, two years after the Porte Saint-Denis, also for Louis XIV, this second triumphal arch creates a grandiose feel to the lively 10th arrondissement. The reliefs include depictions of the king and inscriptions of his victories. It's particularly pretty by night and despite the area being slightly seedy, there are now many hip bars and restaurants around. For a thrill, go to Elachi Indian Eatery (7 rue Faubourg Saint Martin) then head through the back corridor to Bar à Naan – a secret cocktail bar set up like a dining carriage of a train careering through India!

ROTUNDAS

The Temple de l'Amour in the Parc de Vincennes is the work of Paris' chief architect Gabriel Davioud and one of the many attractions he created for the park in 1860 as part of Napoleon lll's plan to draw Parisians into the open air to enjoy nature. Its romantic symmetry and stone columns resemble Marie Antoinette's neo-classically-styled Temple de l'Amour in the Petit Trianon in Versailles, which was designed by her

The Temple de la Sybile. Ruby Boukabou

favourite architect, Richard Mique in 1778. Davioud's temple is perched above a man-made grotto overlooking the lake and creates a sense of serenity.

The Temple de la Sybille is another of Davioud's masterpieces inspired by the 1st century BC Roman Temple of Vesta in Tivoli, Italy, with thick ribbed columns and a central inner altar. Sybille was an oracle and priestess of Apollo in Greek mythology. The 1867 rotunda stands on the Île du Belvédère, a man-made hilly island 50m (165ft) above the lake in the Buttes-Chaumont park.

This is a beautiful spot to take time out from the city bustle, particularly at the end of a walk or jog, and listen to your inner oracle.

Rotonde du Parc Monceau

In 1787 a city wall was erected around Paris with toll houses to collect farmers' tax. The Duke of Chartres commissioned neo-classical architect Claude-Nicolas Ledoux to design the fifty-two toll houses, amongst which is the the elegant rotunda in the Parc Monceau. This circular rotunda, with its high, symmetrical ribbed columns, resembles a Doric temple. Once called the Pavillon de Chartres, the top floor was an apartment for the Duke to look over the garden. In the nineteenth century, Gabriel Davioud topped it off with a stylish dome and closed off the park in front of it with beautiful wrought iron gates that are a particularly lovely sight when exiting Métro Monceau.

Rotonde de la Villette

Place de la Bataille-de-Stalingrad, 75019
https://larotondestalingrad.com

Also designed by Ledoux (1786-1792) as a famers' tax house, this rotunda in the Place de la Bataille-de-Stalingrad, between the above ground Métro line and the canal de L'Ourcq, is particularly striking. A single storey square stone building sits beneath the central symmetrical rotunda, which has columns in pairs beneath arches and small square windows. Two porticos face the front and side of the square, each with eight rectangular pillars. Ledoux was apparently inspired by

The rotunda in Parc Monceau.
Ruby Boukabou

Andrea Palladio, an Italian Renaissance architect, and in particular his 1591 rotunda in Vicenza, Italy.

Today you can pop in for a coffee, wine, a pizza, an art exhibition and on weekends, a dance party!

Rotonde de la Villette.

STREETSCAPES – MÉTRO ENTRANCES & STREET FURNITURE

YOU DON'T NEED to spot the Eiffel Tower in the background of a photo to clock that the location is Paris. The lamp posts, benches, advertising columns, newspaper kiosks, Métro entrances and bouquinistes are all emblematic of the French capital.

Métro Entrances

Paris just wouldn't look right without its Belle Époque Métro entrances. Charles Garnier had proclaimed that the public would only embrace the new metropolitan – developed in preparation for the 1900 World Fair– if the signage was artistic. After a failed design competition, Hector Guimard, an architect and designer from Lyon, was handed the job on the credit of his design of the Art Nouveau apartments Castel Béranger (14 rue Jean de la Fontaine, 75016). Asked to make the entrances as elegant as possible, he came up with an aesthetic that had a softer, more personal feel than the city's uniform Haussmannian architecture.

Métro Monceau entrance/exit. Ruby Boukabou

Green posts were curved, moulded cast iron green 'stems' that referenced nature. Glass fanning awnings (roofed 'édicule' structure) represented the wings of a dragonfly (a recurring Art Nouveau motif) with another model being open aired ('entourage'). Only two original édicule entryways exist in Paris today: Port Dauphine and Abbesses (the latter 'replanted' from Hôtel de Ville). And while one of Châtalet's entrances may seem to be an original, it's actually a replica.

The closed 'entourage' models have two vine-like posts topped with burnt red orbs that represent flower buds (or insect eyes, as you will). The typeface in green, set against a yellow background, is now synonymous with Art Nouveau. A total of 141 entrances were installed between 1900 and 1912. But tastes demand to be nurtured. The reaction was shock, they felt somehow un-French (unsurprisingly Salvador Dali loved them).

Guimard resigned in 1914 and was replaced by architect Joseph Cassien-Bernard, who designed stone neo-classical style entrances (Madeline, Opéra ...). Other entrances with the word 'Métro' in cast iron and the orb lamps were designed by Val d'Osne in the 1920s (Saint-Paul, Le Peletier ...). After the war, simpler signs were favoured, such as a bold red M in a blue circle (Sentier) and others in various colours and materials. To mark the 100th anniversary of the Métro, a colourful beaded contemporary artwork was constructed by Jean-Michel Othoniel as a Métro entrance at the Place Colette exit of Palais-Royal, called the 'Kiosque des noctambules'.

Guimard's signs were saved from destruction in the 1950s when the New York Modern Art Museum bought the disused railings from a Métro entrance, then in 1978, the 86 remaining of the initial 141 were declared historic monuments (Réaumur – Sébastopol, Monceau and many more).

Lamp Posts

If you were travelling through Paris by night in the seventeenth century, you could hire a lantern bearer to weave you through the dark streets. As quaint as this may now sound, it was not affordable to all, and potential danger lurked around each street corner (also the thieves knew that if you could afford a lantern bearer, you were likely to be worth robbing!).

Life changed radically with Louis XIV's introduction of street lanterns in 1667 with glass windows hung from cords

Lamp post at Hôtel de Villle. Ruby Boukabou

in the middle of the streets. In 1745 oil lanterns were attached to posts. Gas

Lamps in Île de la Cité.
Ruby Boukabou

lighting appeared in 1800, in private residences, and in 1817 they lit the Passage des Panoramas. Lighting was introduced on streets including Place du Carrousel, rue de Rivoli, and place Vendôme, and by 1857 on the Grand Boulevards and by major monuments. In 1875 Russian electrical engineer Pavel Yablochkov created arc lamps for the Grands Magasins du Louvre and in 1878, the first electric street lights in Paris arrived for the World Fair, with sixty-four lamps lighting avenue de l'Opéra,

Place d'Etoile and Arc de Triomphe. An International Exposition of Electricity in 1881 was the occasion to show off this invention with many more electric lights on the boulevards. And so Paris became the City of Light!

Today there are various styles of lamp posts around the city, some slim and elegant, others flamboyant and decorative, each with its own charm. There's the single pole (as seen near the Invalides), double armed (Place de la Bastille), box/crown topped (Pont des Arts, Montmartre), rounded (Place des Vosges), 3-armed candelabra style (Place de l'Opéra), 4-armed (Hôtel de Ville), 5-armed candelabra (Louvre) and the ornate Belle Époque style (Pont Alexandre III). Other lamps are attached directly to the façades of buildings (Buttes-aux-Cailles).

Whatever their form, they're iconically Parisian and may inspire you to dance underneath them à la Gene Kelly, or at least have a poetic thought as you pass.

Lights on Pont Alexandra III.

Benches

In the eighteenth century one could hire a seat and so it was a real privilege to sit, rest and watch the world go by. It wasn't until the mid-nineteenth century that benches were installed all over the city, as part of Haussmann's vast public works programme. They were designed to comply with his plan for a unified city with Gabriel Davioud and were green to blend in with other street furniture. The design has remained popular – a simple cast iron base, two parallel wooden planks to sit on and another to support the back.

Plenty of outdoor public seating throughout the city today means that Paris remains an ideal place for the *flâneur* (someone who meanders around town without specific direction) – you can wander around, following your nose, then find a bench for a rest, to read a book or practice some people (and building!) watching. These public benches are particularly convenient when it's sunny but not too hot, as few Parisians have a private garden and many apartments lack natural light. You'll find them in parks, squares, by the Seine and in the centre of the boulevards.

Morris Columns

Advertising posters were once plastered over the public urinals ('pissoirs'). While a somewhat practical use of space, the smelly conditions of consumption were not ideal for selling services or products. A much more tasteful model was created in 1868 by printer Gabriel Morris and his son Richard, winning the City of Paris competition with their 625cm dark green circular billboards with pointed domes decorated with leaves/scales that blended with the other street furniture and trees. Hundreds were erected, including more elaborate models by Gabriel Davioud with 'Spectacles' and 'Théâtre' displayed on a round strip under the awning. While mostly displaying posters for theatrical productions, the columns sometimes also doubled as telephone booths. They are now lit and some rotate, still advertising theatre but also films and other events. 'Wilmotte columns' are the more contemporary version in grey metal, however, they don't quite have the same charm.

Fountains

The earliest fountains in Paris were built to carry water from springs for drinking or washing. One of the oldest fountains was on the corner of rue Saint-Martin and rue Maubée in the 4th arrondissement. It was built in 1392 by Charles VI and carried rather unpleasant-tasting water (through limestone) from Belleville. It was rebuilt in 1733 by Jean Beausire and moved to the corner of rue Saint-Martin and rue de Venise in 1937 (behind where the Pompidou Centre now stands).

In the Jardin du Luxembourg is the beautiful Fontaine Médicis, built in 1630 for

Wallace Fountain in the 13th arrondissement.

Ruby Boukabou

Marie Medici in Italian Renaissance style.

Most of the fountains were monumental and supplied Parisians with drinking water while glorifying Napoleon's campaigns or making grand statements – such as Fontaine du Palmier (1808, Place du Châtelet, 75001) by François-Jean Bralle, with water spurting through the mouths of four sphinxes, sitting under a Romanesque triumphal column (see page 64). Two symbolic 1840 neo-classical fountains in Place de la Concorde by Jacques Ignace Hittorff captured some of the overflow water from Canal de L'Ourcq: the north honouring the rivers, and the south, the seas. Inspired by monumental Roman fountains, they display cast iron figures representing the spirits of maritime navigation and the rivers and produce of France.

The Wallace fountains were financed by English philanthropist Richard Wallace, who sketched designs for sculptor Charles-Auguste Lebourg to perfect. Their constructions aimed to lift morale after the defeat in the Franco-Prussian War and the Paris Commune's destruction of most aqueducts and sources of drinking water. As a humanitarian, Wallace saw the need to provide free drinking water, which was dearer than alcohol and often out of reach of the poor (it was cheaper to get drunk than to stay hydrated!). To stay faithful to the Renaissance style, they had to be useful, beautiful and symbolic. Made of cast iron in dark green to match Paris' other street furniture, they feature four caryatids facing outwards and holding the top of the fountain. These robed women represent simplicity, kindness, charity, and, appropriately, sobriety. The first one was constructed in 1875 and was a huge success.

They stop functioning from 15 November to 15 March to avoid frost damage and *oui*, you can still drink the water! You can find large Wallace fountains all over town and while they were originally green, in 2011 the mayor of the 13th arrondissement decided to modernise their look by having them repainted in red, yellow and pink (you'll also find red ones in Gambetta and blue ones in Belleville).

Find the fountains and take a self-guided fountain walking tour! **https://wallacefountains.org/**.

Other Fountains

Fontaine Stravinsky (rue Brisemiche, 75004) is a cheerful work created in 1983 by Jean Tinguely and Niki de Saint Phalle as a tribute to composer Igor Stravinsky, said to represent how his music sounds. It sits beneath the Pompidou Centre and you will pass it in the Marais walking tour (see page 188).

New fountains were installed about halfway between the Tuileries and the Arc de Triomphe in 2019. Designed by brothers Roman and Erwan Bouroullec, they consist of tall slender crystal studded LED-lit poles representing swirling traffic and have an ethereal quality.

Newspaper Kiosks

Newspaper kiosks were another Gabriel Davioud design, commissioned by Haussmann. Before radio, television and the internet, these stands were the main points of information from the outside world. Again in dark green, they were box-shaped metallic structures with pointed dome roofs situated by Métro entrances and along the boulevards. Plastic versions were created in the 1980s with domes added for nineteenth century aesthetics, but their raison d'etre was threatened in the dawn of the twenty-first century with the decline of the printed press. In 2011, the City of Paris helped save the businesses by allowing a wider range of commerce such as souvenirs, drinks and umbrellas, and invested €200,000 in their upkeep. In 2019 the kiosks began to be replaced by glass and aluminium flat-roofed kiosks, but were called 'ugly sardine cans' by many locals and petitions circulated. The City of Paris promised to maintain thirty-nine of the 1980s' versions (which reference the originals). 'The printed press is a creature of the street', said a former editor of *Le Monde* after a kiosk was burnt down during street protests. 'Each kiosquier defends a little corner of democracy.'

Bouquinistes

The bouquinistes create an original and authentic part of life in Paris. Historic and literary heritage via old books, posters and trinkets can be bought from small green boxes set up along the riverside by passionate collectors.

The profession began in the sixteenth century, but the authorities were dubious about the possibilities of tax evasion in such a business. In 1649 stalls were banned

Bouquiniste Cyril Graffin.

on the Pont Neuf but temporary stands continued to thrive. In 1859 restrictions were relaxed – the bouquinistes were allowed to set up and stay in one location for an annual fee. In 1930 the stands were physically fixed. Today, a few hundred bouquinistes operate over around 900 boxes that are designated UNESCO world heritage sites. You're likely to meet the charming bouquiniste Cyril Graffin on the Bridges Walking tour (quai des Grands Augustins, near the corner of Pont Neuf) so you can say bonjour and ask him any questions you have about this quaint profession! (see page 184)

Public Toilets

Outdoor free-standing public toilets exist in Paris in the form of long grey oblongs that house one toilet. They double as walls for maps of the local area. If the automatic doors make you nervous though, or if you don't come across one (they're a little few and far between), do like most Parisians and pop into a café to use the utilities. You're expected to consume, but you can just grab a cheap coffee or a Perrier at the bar. Be warned, however, that the French designs don't always consider privacy and the urinals are not always closed off from the female toilet/s, which can be a little uncomfortable if you're not used to it.

CHURCHES AND OTHER PLACES OF WORSHIP

WHILE FRANCE TODAY is a secular country, for centuries the country was officially Catholic and so churches provided the vast population with buildings in which to congregate, nourish their spirituality and assuage their fears. With this in mind, you should be able to appreciate visiting some of the many churches of Paris, whatever your religion. There are over 200 in the city, many with sublime architecture and art. Most are free to enter (unless indicated). They also provide beautiful respite from the cacophony of the Parisian streets.

Why not appreciate the architecture while live music uplifts your spirits?

Check the churches' websites for their regular free organ and choral recitals, often before or after Mass, or visit the Classic Tic website for the schedule of other classical and spiritual music concerts. **www.classictic.com/en/ special/paris_church_concerts**

Sainte-Chapelle

8 Boulevard du Palais, 75001
www.sainte-chapelle.fr/en
(Ticketed or free entry with the Paris Pass and Paris Museum Pass)

Sainte-Chapelle, consecrated in 1248, is a prime example of the Gothic style.

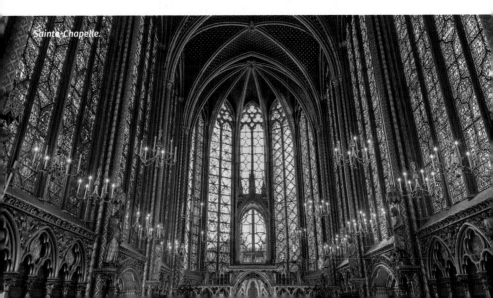

Sainte-Chapelle.

The church was built on the Île de la Cité on the orders of Louis IX to house the purported Crown of Thorns (later moved to Notre-Dame and, since the 2019 fire, held in the Louvre). High ribbed vaults are supported by slim columns, and overall building supports are via ring anchors, iron reinforcements and external buttresses. The lower chapel, with its many columns, was open to commoners to worship, while the upper chapel was exclusive to the Royal Family. The chapel is famous for arguably the most beautiful stained-glass windows in the world, which filter the light through fifteen windows to divine, kaleidoscopic effects (recitals here are magical). The windows of the nave depict scenes from the Old Testament, while the eastern apse windows depict the New Testament. On the western wall is a large rose window with flamboyant tracery. Also look out for the scenes of the discovery of the relics of Christ being brought to Paris with King Louis IX on the west of the south windows. Epic and illuminating.

Saint-Eustache

2 Impasse Saint-Eustache, 75001
www.saint-eustache.org

The beauty of Saint-Eustache is in its multiple personalities from its fusion of Gothic, Renaissance and classical styles. Begun in 1532, the 50m-high basilica with five naves wasn't consecrated until 1637. Gothic elements include the tracery windows (ornate stonework supporting the glass) and high vaulted ceilings. A classical-styled façade was added in 1754–1788. Restorations took place in 1840, then more recently from 2016–2018. The church boasts the biggest pipe organ in France so if you are around

Saint-Eustache.

on a Sunday afternoon, you may like to attend a free recital from 5.30pm to 6pm. Also check their site for other concerts from The National Orchestra and the Radio France Concert Choir.

Saint-Roch

296 rue Saint-Honoré, 75001
www.paroissesaintroch.fr

Louis XIV laid the cornerstone to the Saint-Roch parish church in 1653. The building was first designed by Jacques Lemercier, but not completed until 1754 to what are thought to be the plans of Jules Hardouin-Mansart. The three-nave basilica combines a Gothic plan, classical details (including an Italian influenced engaged column) and Baroque sensibilities (decorative flourishes and a painted dome). Diderot and Le Nôtre are among those who were buried here.

Saint- Roch.

Notre-Dame

6 Parvis Notre-Dame – Pl. Jean-Paul II, 75004
www.notredamedeparis.fr/en

In 1663 Maurice de Sully, the bishop of Paris, laid the foundation stone of 'our lady' cathedral in the presence of Pope Alexander III. His ambitious project was to take place at no random location, but at the symbolic and geographical heart of Paris, the Île de la Cité, on the foundations of two earlier churches and the site of a Gallo-Roman temple dedicated to Jupiter. Inspired by Saint-Denis Basilica (see page 104), Sully aimed to out-do Abbot Suger and impress the rest of the world with the immense height and superb details in his cathedral. Indeed, it soon became, and has remained, the world's finest example of Gothic architecture alongside Saint Chapelle. The roof is 35m (115ft) high and the interior is 130m by 48m (427 by 157ft); the plan, one of a five-aisle basilica though longer with wide aisles, square chapels and a fourth storey with circular windows. High ribbed vaults are supported by compound piers. Coherence, space and flow was of primary importance, creating a sense of space and awe.

The imposing and iconic twin towers, inspired by Syria's Qalb Lozeh fifth-century church, were completed in 1250, creating a stunning symmetrical western front (main entrance) with doors decorated with carvings and figures of the kings from the Old Testament. You

View from the rear of the bullding, before the fire.

Similiar view to above showing the fire damage.

can spend hours just gazing at these details alone. On the west, the flying buttresses are both functional (allowing more internal space with high columns) and decorative (producing a proud and bold quality). Gargoyles served as both drainage of rain water and to ward off evil spirits (the current ones are nineteenth-century recreations). The rose stained-glass windows with radial tracery are marvels, also inspired by Syrian architecture.

In 1708 the choir was adapted in the glory of the Virgin on the orders of Louis XIV, then in 1793 the cathedral was looted by revolutionaries and renamed the Temple of Reason. Another transformation took place when Napoleon stepped in and brought religion back, restoring the building in which he crowned himself as Emperor, alongside his Empress Josephine, in 1804. The ceremony was immortalised by Jacques-Louis David in his 1807 painting, 'The Coronation of Napoleon' that hangs in the Louvre.

Soon after, however, the church fell into disrepair, saved only by a public relations stunt of sorts when in 1831, Victor Hugo's novel *The Hunchback of Notre Dame*, a beauty and the beast scenario between the hunchbacked

Jacques-Louis David 1807 painting The Coronation of Napoleon.

View from the bell tower.

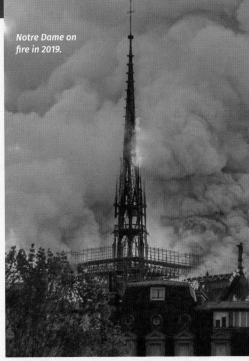

Notre Dame on fire in 2019.

bell-ringer Quasimodo and a beautiful Gypsy girl called Esmeralda, successfully created international interest in the cathedral and a renewed fascination with the Middle Ages. This resulted in public rallies for the monument's restoration and both local and international finances. Architect Eugène Emmanuel Viollet-le-Duc led a major restoration project and repaired the gargoyles, replaced missing statues and raised a new spire.

The cathedral continued to thrive as Paris' major landmark and a place of worship and ceremony. In 1909 Joan of Arc was beatified (a belated apology for her being burnt at the stake by mistake!) and the funeral of President Mitterrand took place here in 1996.

The French government contributed millions of euros for maintenance annually and Notre-Dame remained a number one attraction, in particular the climb to the bell tower for panoramic views.

During restoration in 2019 a fire broke out and soon the whole world was watching in shock as the flames raged, smoke billowed and the roof and spire collapsed. The Paris fire brigade became overnight heroes when making a human chain to reach inside and put out the flames, saving most of the building including the organ, the rose windows and the purported Crown of Thorns (now in the Louvre). The upper walls were severely damaged and the fire and water damage was extensive. While President Macron almost immediately proclaimed to rebuild the cathedral in five years, experts say it will take much longer.

Saint-Paul-Saint-Louis.

Saint-Paul-Saint-Louis

99 rue St. Antoine, 75004
www.spsl.fr

Financed by Louis XIII, this Baroque church was built in the Marais between 1627 and 1641. Breaking from the Gothic trend, it combined Roman and classical French architectural plans by Jesuit architects Étienne Martellange and François Derand. Architectural influences include the Gesù in Rome (the 1584 Jesuit church with similar but smaller side chapels and a single nave), and Saint-Gervais-Saint-Protais (for the bays and columns on the façade), Italian Baroque (the dome above the crossing) and French Gothic style (the height of the dome at 55m/180ft). Cardinal Richelieu celebrated the first Mass here in 1641. Leave through the side exit to discover a cute cobblestoned laneway.

Saint-Gervais-Saint-Protais

13 rue des Barres, 75004
https://paris.fraternites-jerusalem.org

Another church in the Marais that's a beautiful respite from the hustle and bustle, just east of the City Hall, is Saint-Gervais-Saint-Protais Church, named after two Christian martyrs from Milan. Construction started in 1494 in Gothic style but by the time they reached the façade, a new style was being born and so this became one of the first of the

Saint-Gervais-Saint-Protais.

French Baroque-styled buildings (with elaborate and ornamental details to create a wow factor), with the foundation stone placed in 1616 by a young Louis XIII. Inside, the carved choir stalls date back to medieval times and the beautiful stained-glass windows from the sixteenth century. The original organ remains.

Saint-Louis-en-l'Île

19 rue Saint-Louis en l'Île, 75004
www.saintlouisenlile.catholique.fr

This Catholic church was named after Louis IX (1226–1270,) who was known to come to the city island to pray. Plans were laid out by François Le Vau (brother of Louis Le Vau) and construction took place from 1664 to

1726. The Baroque architecture has some Gothic accents as well as a 'modern' slant – that is to say that the new trend was Italian influences but adapted to France. The bell tower dates from 1741.

Saint-Merri

76 rue de la Verrerie, 75004

After visiting the Pompidou Centre, sneak into the side entrance of Saint-Merri for a change of atmosphere. This parish church was constructed between 1500 and 1550 in flamboyant Gothic style and holds an eighteenth-century organ played by Camille Saint-Saëns, the organist here from 1853–1857 (if you have your headphones, his

Saint-Merri.

Façade of Saint-Merri. Ruby Boukabou

compositions could be an appropriate soundtrack to your virtual or physical visit!). A lovely little side chapel with black and white checked tiles is lit by three skylights and decorated with large allegorical paintings. Exit from

the front to marvel at the frieze of intricate carved angels, figures and the gargoyles. The church holds regular visual art exhibitions drawing attention to inequality, and other events.

Saint-Étienne-du-Mont

Place Sainte-Geneviève, 75005
www.saintetiennedumont.fr

This parish church dedicated to the patron saint of Paris, St Geneviève, is amongst Paris' finest. Construction took place between 1492 and 1622 on the site of a previous church. The three-level wedding-cake structure, typical of the Middle Ages, has a Gothic pinnacle and a high bell-tower. The doorway resembles a Greek temple with columns and decorations of St Stephen's martyrdom. Inside there's so much to admire, from the golden lamps, to the shrine of St Geneviève to Paris' only remaining rood screen or 'jube' (ornate partition between the chancel and nave) over two spiral staircases. Playwright Jean Racine and physicist Blaise Pascal were buried here.

Saint-Julien-le-Pauvre

79 rue Galande, 75005
www.sjlpmelkites.com

Saint-Julien-le-Pauvre is considered one of the oldest churches in Paris, built in 1165 but dating back even earlier in another form. It fuses Romanesque and early Gothic styles and houses a paving stone from the original Roman road from Lutetia (Paris) to Orléans. Intimate and peaceful, it is also a lovely place to just sit quietly or attend a piano recital. Since 1889 it has been an Eastern Catholic Melkite church.

Saint-Séverin

3 rue des Prêtres Saint-Séverin, 75005
https://saint-severin.com

Saint-Séverin was built in the thirteenth century on the foundations of a possible sixth-century church, itself above the grave of Severinus, a hermit. Flamboyant elements include its twisted columns. Some of the stained-glass windows here date back to the fourteenth century. The organ concerts are famous.

Val-de-Grâce Abbey

1 Place Alphonse Laveran, 75005
http://valdegrace.org/
Tuesday–Thursday, Saturday–Sunday 12–6pm. Guided tour by appointment: +33 (0) 1 40 51 51 92
Passport or identity card needed to pass security. Ring the bell on the right edge of the front gate and pay the small entrance fee.

To thank God for the birth of an heir to the throne, Anne of Austria commissioned François Mansart to

Val-de-Grâce Abbey.

build the Val-de-Grâce Abbey, and the foundation stone was later laid by the young heir himself – Louis XIV. Mansart created a bold, captivating portico entrance and fused influences from Rome (the dome) with French Baroque classical style (the choir and nave plan) and twisted marble columns. However, he went way over budget so Jacques Lemercier was brought in to complete the building.

Used as a military hospital after the Revolution, it now includes a museum dedicated to the French military medical service, the Museum of the Armed Forces Health Service.

The small square in front is particularly charming.

Saint-Sulpice

2 rue Palatine, 75006
https://pss75.fr/saint-sulpice-paris/

In 1646 Anne of Austria laid the cornerstone of this beautiful parish church that was built for the field workers to plans by Christophe Gamard, and later by Daniel Gittard. Saint-Sulpice was built on the site of a thirteenth-century Romanesque church and is the second largest church in Paris, located close to the Luxembourg

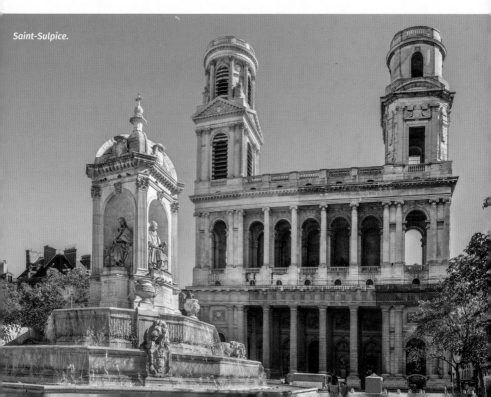

Saint-Sulpice.

The interior of Saint-Sulpice.

Gardens on the Left Bank. The floor plan resembled Notre-Dame and flying buttresses support the choir. The theatrical elegance is in the façade, with two towers, a double portico and monumental classical columns by Giovanni Niccolò Servandoni (aka Jean-Nicolas Sevran), a Florence-born architect, decorator and set designer whose father was French. His inspirations included St Paul's Cathedral in London. Inside you'll find original murals by Romantic master Eugène Delacroix, including 'Jason Wrestling with the Angel' and 'Heliodorus Driven from the Temple'. The church featured in the 2003 film *The Da Vinci Code*.

Saint-Germaine-des-Prés

3 Place Saint-Germain des Prés, 75006
www.eglise-saintgermaindespres.fr

King Childebert, son of Clovis l, founded this church and monastery in 543. It became the final resting place for the Merovingian kings and was renamed after Germanus, the canonised bishop of Paris who had consecrated the church. The building has the oldest church tower in the city, which was reconstructed from 1000 to 1163, after being ransacked by the Vikings. The philosopher René Descartes was buried here and, along with the nearby Sorbonne, it held a breathtaking array of literature and manuscripts. Then came the Revolution and its aftermath, leaving the church 'unsalvageable'. Victor Hugo and others lobbied until Victor Baltard and painter Jean Hippolyte Flandrin set about a major restoration in 1840. In 2016 another restoration began on the severely deteriorated building, mostly funded by private donors, with the City of Paris putting in 15 per cent.

The American Church in Paris

65 quai d'Orsay, 75007
www.acparis.org

In 1857 a church was built on rue de Berri, near the Champs-Élysées, to accommodate the American community in Paris. It was the first American church to be built outside the United States. The current church, built 1926–1931 in the 7th arrondissement, now welcomes all Anglophone communities. The building is based on a fifteenth-century plan in Gothic style. The interiors include carved Hungarian oaks and Italian marble floor and altar. Check the site for tour times and to find out

about concerts by talented musicians of various nationalities.

Holy Trinity Cathedral and the Russian Orthodox Spiritual and Cultural Centre

1 quai Branly, 75007
https://cathedrale-sainte-trinite.fr
Visits – 2pm–7pm
Exhibition at the cultural centre:
Tuesday-Sunday, 2pm–7pm

You can't miss this 2016-built Russian Orthodox Church by the Seine for its five golden onion-shaped domes with 90,000 golden leaves and a Russian Orthodox cross. The complex is built with a variety of materials, including Massangis stone from Burgundy, and concrete. Enter to be mesmerised by the golden chandelier, artworks and decorations.

Saint-Louis, Cathedral Dôme des Invalides

129 rue de Grenelle, 75007
www.musee-armee.fr/en

Les Invalides is a complex of museums and monuments themed around French military history. The original purpose was a home, hospital and church for war veterans, established in 1670 by Louis XIV. Saint-Louis Cathedral was designed by a young Jules Hardouin-Mansart, the double columns and other neo-classical features inspired by Rome's St Peter's. The church had seperate sections for veterans and royalty. The veteran's chapel has a classical plan

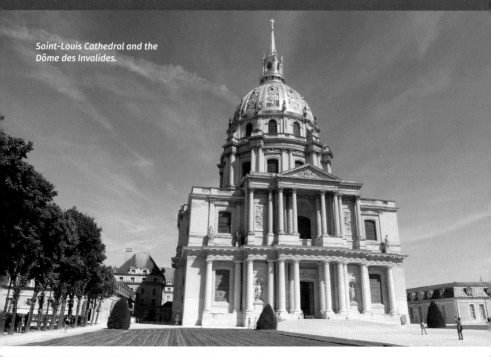

*Saint-Louis Cathedral and the
Dôme des Invalides.*

while the royal section, for the exclusive use of Louis XIV and his entourage (and for royal tombs), had something much more elaborate - a spectacular royal chapel, the "Dôme des Invalides". It is a seventeenth-century architectural gem, the epitome of French Baroque and remains one of Paris' most impressive architectural attractions. The 107m-high dome was wrapped in gold leaf, gilded in 1706 and restored in 1989. It is, literally, a brilliant landmark. The interior fresco by Charles de La Fosse illustrates Louis X offering his sword to Christ. In the nineteenth century, an excavation took place under the dome to create a crypt for the tomb of Napoleon, designed by French/Italian architect Louis-Tullius-Joachim Visconti and constucted in red quartzite and green granite. It can be visited as part of the Musée de l'Armée (the Army Museum).

La Madeleine

Place de la Madeleine, 75008
www.eglise-lamadeleine.com

The Madeleine, designed by Pierre-Alexandre Vignon in 1806, was named after Mary Magdalene and inspired by ancient Roman temples, in particular the smaller but spectacularly preserved Maison Carrée temple in Nîmes, in the south of France. It sits nobly in the centre of Haussmannian Paris with a prominent Corinthian colonnade

La Madeleine.

consisting of fifty-two 20m (66ft) high columns that surround the entire building. The church was originally intended as a temple of glory for the French Army, but instead, the Arc de Triomphe de L'Étoile was built. Unlike most churches in Paris, it has no clock tower or external crosses, but a pediment with a sculpture of the Last Judgement, by neo-classical sculptor Philippe Joseph Henri Lemaire, and bronze doors with reliefs of the Ten Commandments. The interiors of the single nave church were designed by Jean-Jacques Huvé and inspired by Roman baths and Renaissance artists. Look out for the statue of Mary Magdalene being lifted up by angels, above the high altar, and the frescoes above 'L'Histoire du Christianisme' (The History of Christianity) by artist Jules-Clause Ziegler. The 1845, fifty-eight-stop organ is one of the largest in Paris. Le Lavage de La Madeleine is a Brazilian festival that is celebrated here in September. Flowers, Brazilian rhythms and French and Portuguese chatter transform the forecourt.

Alexander Nevsky Cathedral

12 rue Daru, 75008
www.cathedrale-orthodoxe.com

This major 1861 neo-byzantine, Moscow-styled Russian Orthodox church was the first Russian Orthodox place of worship in France. Memorable past events include the wedding of Pablo Picasso and Russian dancer Olga Khokhlova in 1918, and the funeral of painter Wassily Kandinsky in 1944. It is also famous for its exceptional choir. The five spires are tipped with golden cupolas and the interior highlight is the central high Russian dome and its red and gold colour scheme.

Notre-Dame-de-l'Arche-d'Alliance

81 rue d'Alleray 75015
www.ndarche.org

Designed by Architecture Studio (most famous for The Arab World Institute alongside Jean Nouvel), this contemporary and innovative church amongst the high rise 1970s' buildings in the 15th arrondissement represents a more subtle way of worshipping in what is now a secular country. A sober alluminium spire holds a small cross and a bell that indicates the building's function that is not obvious on first glance. Steel mesh surrounds an 18m cube, whose equal sides symbolise the unity of God. Twelve pillars reference the apostles and the tribes of Israel.

Inside the plan represents a Greek cross and the wood panelling represents the Ark of the Convenant, from which the church takes its name, the wooden chest that featured in the Book of Exodus and is said to have contained the Ten Commandments on stone tablets. Stained-glass windows depict Mary's visitation to Elisabeth when she was pregnant with John the Baptist.

The building was consecrated in 1998 and in 2012 received a twentieth-century heritage listing.

Saint-Jean de Montmartre

21 rue des Abbesses, 75018
www.saintjeandemontmartre.com

The 1890s saw a new trend in Paris constructions with reinforced concrete that allowed building on a steeply sloping site. At the foot of Montmartre, Saint-Jean de Montmartre church was one of the first examples of this, built by architect Anatole de Baudot between 1894 and 1904 with the engineering system of Paul Cottancin. Material was needed that was lightweight and easy to produce and the technique of using reinforced concrete was so new that technical demonstrations needed to be made to counteract an order for demolition in 1902. The Art Nouveau redbrick façade sits handsomely opposite the Abbesses Métro station, which also showcases Nouveau architecture with its station exit.

Saint-Jean de Montmartre.

Sacré-Coeur Basilica

35 rue du Chevalier de la Barre, 75018
www.sacre-coeur-montmartre.com

Perched majestically on top of the Montmartre hill is Paris' most iconic and romantic architectural building, the Sacré-Coeur Basilica. In Roman times, a temple for Mars and Mercury stood here, and when you visit you'll understand why the spot is so special – at the highest point in Paris, it's literally the closest place you can get to the planets, and to God. Not to mention the exceptionally inspiring vistas in all directions.

Construction of Sacré-Coeur began in 1871 after the defeat of France in the Franco-Prussian War the previous year. The Parisians were gloomy (or else drunk!) and the basilica was a symbol of repentance to God and of hope for a better future. Finance came from the faithful whose names are engraved in the walls.

The original architect was Paul Abadie, whose plans were inspired by a multi-domed seventeenth-century Romanesque cathedral he had restored in the south of France, in Perigueux (Dordogne), Saint-Front, whose influences included Hagia Sofia in Constantinople/Instanbul (c.537), San Marco in Venice (consecrated in 832) and possibly India's Taj Mahal.

The neo-romano-byzantine building has a square plan with four cupolas and a dome, while its most stand-out feature is the luminous white colour of the basilica created from the Château-Landon stones that naturally wash themselves and expel pollution when in contact with water. Other external features to look out for include a triple-arched portico, elegant equestrian bronze statues of French national saints Joan of Arc and King Louis IX, and the 19 tonne 'Savoyarde' bell that arrived in 1895 from Annecy, dragged by twenty-one horses.

Inside, the floor plan is typical of a basilica in the shape of a Greek cross, with the dome sitting over the crossing. The choir loft is exceptionally large and features an awe-inspiring ceiling mosaic of Christ, to whom the basilica is dedicated. Luc-Olivier Merson's all engulfing artwork depicts Christ, arms spread open and wearing a white robe through which glows a golden heart. The choice of blue and gold in the mosaic is one of the building's Islamic architecture influences, as are the double domes and arcades of trefoil arches, as pointed out by Diana Darke in her book *Stealing from the Saracens*.

The basilica was completed with several other architects such as Lucien Magne (1905-1916). While almost completed in 1914, it was not consecrated until 1919, as a result of the First World War. Climb the bell tower for an incredible panorama of Paris, but even from the steps in front there's a terrific view, particularly spectacular at sunset.

Sacré-Coeur.

Saint-Pierre de Montmartre

2 rue du Mont-Cenis, 75018
www.saintpierredemontmartre.net

Not far from Sacré-Coeur and Place du Tertre artist square, but easy to miss, Saint-Pierre de Montmartre is worth a visit when in the area. It is built on the site of a Roman temple dedicated to Mars and dates back to 1147, joining Saint-Julien-le-Pauvre as one of the oldest surviving Paris churches. The building combines Romanesque architecture with early Gothic form. Stained-glass windows depicting Bible stories include vignettes of the life of Peter the Apostle (added in 1953 by Max Ingrand).

Notre-Dame-de-la-Croix de Ménilmontant

3 Place de Ménilmontant, 75020
www.notredamedelacroix.com

This picturesque church in the backstreets of Ménilmontant has various personalities depending on which angle you approach it from – vertical, elegant and slender from beneath and round and voluptuous from the side. Architect Louis-Jean-Antoine Héret chose a neo-Medieval meets neo-Romanesque style, with elements of modernity including the use of exposed cast iron. Construction took place between 1863 and 1880. The church was used for political meetings by the Paris Commune and features

Notre-Dame-de-la-Croix de Ménilmontant. Ruby Boukabou

in the film *L'Écume des Jours* starring Romain Duris and Audrey Tautou.

Saint-Denis Basilica

1 rue de la Légion d'Honneur, 93200 Saint-Denis
www.saint-denis-basilique.fr/en/
(Ticketed)
*Saint-Denis is a northern suburb of Paris. The RER train will get you there in less than half an hour from Châtalet, then it's a 10-15 minute walk. Métro (line 13) and busses service the area as well, but will take a little longer, depending on where you're coming from.

While Saint-Denis is outside of central Paris, it is worth the trip for the architectural significance of the basilica and the Royal necropolis.

In 623 the sanctuary became a church under Merovingian King Dagobert I, replacing Saint-Germaine-des-Prés as the royal crypt.

In the twelfth century, architect Abbot Suger, under Louis VII, made history by adapting the Carolingian style building 'inventing' Gothic architecture inspired by the writings of fifth cenutury

Saint-Denis Basilica.

Syrian mystic philosopher, Denys, on how to induce uplifting, spiritual experiences for the (mostly illiterate) public through architecture with height, space and, most importantly, light. Suger externalised the structure of the building, creating room for large windows that allowed light to flow in, which represented a divine presence, particularly with the help of stained-glass. Radiating chapels and double pitched roofs were constructed to allow even more light through high windows and to create fluid and unified spaces. The building was consecrated in 1144 and became a major influence on architectural styles throughout Medieval Europe. It is still considered one of the world's most significant monuments.

Check their site for entrance fee, opening hours and and exhibitions.

Notre-Dame de Pentecôte

1 avenue de la Division Leclerc, 92800 Puteaux
https://ndp92.fr

Notre-Dame de Pentecôte was built in Paris' business district in 2001 to serve as a place where people could escape the chaotic city life and find peace and silence. Architect Franck Hammoutène sought to avoid a strong contrast with other buildings in La Défense and it therefore resembles a contemporary and slick office building. It's not a parish church, but rather a space where people can relax and pray.

Grande Mosquée de Paris.

Other Places of Worship
Grande Mosquée de Paris

2bis Place du Puits de l'Ermite, 75005
www.mosqueedeparis.net
Visits 9am–12 noon and 2pm–7pm except Fridays.

Make sure to have shoulders and knees covered, and, if you're a woman, a scarf to wrap loosely over your head as a sign of respect. A token entrance fee of a few euros is requested.

Inaugurated in 1926 as a token of gratitude to the Muslim tirailleurs (colonial infantrymen), the Hispano-Moorish mosque was designed by architect Maurice Tranchant de Lunel in neo-mudejar style. It is one of the oldest and largest mosques in France. During the Second World War it served as a secret refuge for North African, and some say European, Jews, providing shelter, safe passage and fake passports. With its beautiful green and white tiled 33m minaret it's to be appreciated, not just by those worshipping, but by all. If you're visiting in winter and are female, thaw out in the hammam, the traditional and beautiful bathhouse. Everyone can enjoy mint tea and delicious sweet pastries in the courtyard café paved with mosaics, or a couscous in the restaurant with continuous service from lunch to dinner.

Grande Synagogue de Paris

44 rue de la Victoire, 75009
www.lavictoire.org

Also known as the Synagogue de la Victoire, the official seat of the chief rabbi of Paris and place of worship for the Jewish community, was designed by architect Alfred-Philibert Aldrophe and inaugurated in 1874. It boasts a Romanesque facade with Byzantine features. Inside are balconies, candelabras, numerous religious inscriptions and stained-glass windows representing the Tribes of Israel.

La Grande Pagode Buddhist Temple

40bis route de Ceinture du Lac Daumesnil, 75012
www.bouddhisme-france.org

The 800m² temple is located in the former 1931 Colonial Exhibition by the lake in the woods of Vincennes, in the former houses of Cameroon and Togo. It was converted into a place of worship in 1977 and restored in 2015. The 9m-tall statue of Buddha is the biggest in Europe. It is open to the public during major Buddhist festivals.

Meditation Space by Tadao Ando

32 avenue de Ségur, 75007
Monday–Friday (9am–6pm)

This unique space was built in 1995 to commemorate the 50th anniversary of the adoption of UNESCO's Constitution. The intention was to create a place where people from around the world, of all races and religions, could pray for peace, reflect on the horrors of Hiroshima and on the destructive power of humankind. The structure is next to the garden in a courtyard. The irradiated granite cylinder from Hiroshima is 6m in diameter and height. Light enters this space from a small slit between the wall. For the project a donation of 10,000 yen (about €70.50 at the time) was requested from individuals in Japan. It raised a total of 140,000,000 yen. The names of the donors can be seen in the interior walls. Tadao is a self-taught architect and has won many prestigious awards.

MUSEUMS

THE BEST PART about admiring the architecture of Paris' museums is that you can also be wowed by the incredible art on offer inside, including depictions of the city throughout the ages as seen and imagined through the brushes, pencils, hands and lenses of artists.

Le Louvre

Rue de Rivoli, 75001
www.louvre.fr/en

Whether you're visiting the museum, or checking out its wonderful virtual experiences, the Louvre is a sight to behold. From fortress to palace to art gallery, it is one of Paris' most iconic buildings. Philippe II constructed the castle and a moat when he was erecting a wall around Paris in the late twelfth century – he wasn't sure that those English folk would stay at bay and didn't want to take any risks. Over the next centuries the castle transformed into a plush palace with various extensions by each king (for example, as part of Henri IV's extensions, a 430m-long gallery was constructed to reach Catherine de Medici's Palais des Tuileries). French and Italian styles were fused through further extensions by architect Pierre Lescot, including an apartment wing in 1549 that was later replaced by a royal courtyard. Claude Perrault added classical columns and a triangular pediment and Louis XIV's quarters were constructed on the eastern side before Versailles became his residence of choice. After the revolution in 1789 and a bloody adieu to the royals, the Louvre transformed into an art gallery, gradually obtaining the world's most impressive collection.

You can easily spend a day in and around the Louvre taking in the details of the various architects over the years. If the crowds get too much, take a stroll around the Tuileries, sit by the banks of the Seine or find respite at Le Meurice hotel bar/café (228 rue de Rivoli, 75001). At home? Visit an exhibition virtually via their website and download the app 'Mona Lisa Beyond the Glass' for a fantastic 360-degree experience with a recreation of Mona Lisa and learn more of her story.

The Louvre Pyramid

Commissioned by President François Mitterrand in 1984, Chinese-American architect I.M. Pei designed the iconic glass and metal pyramid in the courtyard of the Louvre. Lit up after dark, the 21m-high pyramid proves a stunning 'Paris by night' shot. As with the Pompidou Centre and the Eiffel Tower, it was much criticised but is now embraced and understandably so – it gives the square a magical touch.

Le Louvre.

The Louvre Pyramid.

Musée de l'Orangerie

Jardin des Tuileries, 75001
+33 (0)1 44 50 43 00
www.musee-orangerie.fr/en

The Musée de l'Orangerie was commissioned by Napoleon III in 1852 to shelter the orange trees of the Tuileries Palace during the harsh winters. The greenhouse allowed sun and light to enter from the southern façade (facing the Seine), while there are no windows on the northern side so as to protect the tress from the wind chill. The entrances on the west and east are topped with classical pediments. The building now houses Impressionist and post-Impressionist works, with Monet's 'Water Lilies' as the star attraction.

Musée Picasso

5 rue de Thorigny, 75003
+33 1 85 56 00 36
www.museepicassoparis.fr/en

In 1659 a private mansion was built in the Marais for a salt-tax farmer. Today it is considered the finest historical house in the Marais. The asymmetrical building is in 'Mazarin' style: Italian Baroque combined with neo-classicism beautified with sculptured cupids and sphinxes, Corinthian pilasters, stucco and stone décor and a large central staircase. It was bought by the City of Paris and listed a Historical Monument in 1968. The mansion includes the creation of an internal modernist box to form various

Musée Picasso and the staircase (right) . Fabien Campoverde

spaces via ramps and mezzanines for the extended collection. Lose yourself in literally thousands of works by the Spanish father of Modernism, then explore the cobbled laneways of the Marais with renewed inspiration.

Musée Carnavalet

16 rue des Francs Bourgeois, 75003
+33 (0)1 44 59 58 58
www.carnavalet.paris.fr/en

The Carnavalet Museum delves into the history of Paris and occupies two mansions: the Hôtel Carnavalet (c.1560) and the former Hôtel Le Peletier de Saint-Fargeau (1688). Visit the architectural department to scrutinise Paris' iconic and historic buildings, including those which have been demolished. You'll visit this museum in the Marais walking tour.

Musée Cognacq-Jay

8 rue Elzevir, 75003
+33 (0)1 40 27 07 21
www.museecognacqjay.paris.fr

Médéric de Donon had this private mansion constructed in c.1575, and lived in it for the rest of his life. Its style set a trend. Surrounding a central, rectangular courtyard the *hôtel particulier* (grand town house) is made up of two main wings: the south for stables, and later garages, and the north as a single, long gallery with evenly placed windows creating a sense of order. The arched windows and pediment on the roof of the corps de logis are

examples of the classical Roman influences and the high beamed ceiling on the top floor is remarkably still intact. Seventeenth-century renovations likely included the current street façade and white and gold painted wooden panels in the grand reception room on the ground floor.

The museum houses the private collection of eighteenth century European art of Ernest Cognacq and his wife Marie-Louise Jay, the founders of La Samaritaine department store.

Musée d'Art et d'Histoire du Judaïsme

71 rue du Temple, 75003
www.mahj.org/en

The Museum of Jewish Art and History is housed in the Hôtel de Saint-Aignan. Originally a *hôtel particulier*, it was built between 1644 and 1650 by Pierre Le Muet for Claude de Mesmes, Count of Avauxand. The residence was atypically placed back from the street, behind a large courtyard, and a false façade mirroring the right wing was added to create symmetry. Saved by the City of Paris in 1962 as part of their scheme to preserve the Marais, the museum focuses on Jewish communities from the Middle Ages to the beginning of the twentieth century.

Musée de la Chasse et de la Nature

62 rue des Archives, 75003
+33 (0)1 53 01 92 40
www.chassenature.org

This 'hunting and nature' museum traces

some traditions and practices of hunting while presenting a contemporary art programme. It occupies two private mansions, the Hôtel de Guénégaud (1655, François Mansart) built for the king's secretary Jean-François de Guénégaud des Brosses and the neighbouring Hôtel de Mongelas, constructed in the early eighteenth century.

La Gaîté Lyrique

3bis rue Papin, 75003
+33 (0)1 53 01 52 00
https://gaite-lyrique.net/en

La Gaîté Lyrique was a 1862 Belle Époque theatre transformed into a digital cultural hub in 2010. Their focus is on wonder, learning and transmission through digital arts, music, cinema, graphic design and video games.
The façade, foyer and entrance are reminders of its original glory.

Musée des Arts et Métiers

60 rue Réaumur, 75003
+33 (0)1 53 01 82 00
www.arts-et-metiers.net

This museum in the Marais, dedicated to science and technology innovations in France, is located in one of Paris' longest standing churches, the former monastery of Saint-Martin-des-Champs, which dates back to c.1060. It was a precursor to the Gothic style with vault supports and flying buttresses, and the chapels were combined to create a single space with columns.

Be hypnotised by Foucault's original pendulum, a device the inventor used in 1851 to prove that the earth rotates.

Centre Pompidou

Place Georges-Pompidou, 75004
+33 (0)1 44 78 12 33
www.centrepompidou.fr/en

This modern art cultural centre by architects Renzo Piano and Richard Rogers, inaugurated in 1977, was, and still is, seen as revolutionary: the escalators, ducts and colour-coded engineering workings are placed outside of the building and are visible from afar. The blue represents moving air (air conditioning); yellow: circulating electricity; green: circulating water, and red: moving people (escalators and lifts). The transparency of the façade, the galleries and especially the escalators snaking their way up the side of the building are a revelation – a flexible, functional, transparent, inside-out mechanism. While some originally considered it an eyesore, it's become

a beloved part of Paris' skyline and widely adored, particularly by architects who admire that despite the passing decades, it has continued to feel modern. The building has ten floors of 7,500 m² that are adaptable in form and the top floor boasts a panoramic view.

The Pompidou Centre houses the Musée National d'Art Moderne with works from 1905 to the present day, a large library, bookshop, cinema, a children's workshop, an audio-visual section and a panoramic restaurant – Le George. The square below is a constant buzz with portrait painters, buskers and terraced cafés.

Maison de Victor Hugo

6 Place des Vosges, 75004
+33 (0)1 42 72 10 16
http://maisonsvictorhugo.paris.fr/en

After visiting the first planned square in Paris – Henri IV's Place Royale (now the Place des Vosges) – enter the surrounding redbrick court-like building. On the second floor at number six is where Victor Hugo lived and wrote between 1832 and 1848. Check out his furniture, sketches, memorabilia, writing desk, collection of porcelain and pictures. Hopefully you'll leave inspired, not *misérable*.

Institut du Monde Arabe

1 rue des Fossés Saint-Bernard, 75005
www.imarabe.org

Designed by French 'starchitect' Jean Nouvel, with Architecture-Studio (Martin Robain, Rodo Tisnado, Jean-François Bonne, Jean-François Galmiche), Gilbert Lèzenes, and Pierre Soria, the Arab World Institute was the result of a joint funding from the Arab States and France with the ambition of encouraging

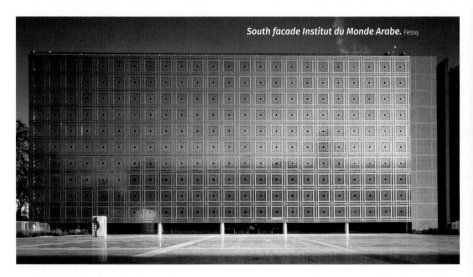

South facade Institut du Monde Arabe. Fessy

dialogue between the cultures. Steel, aluminium and glass materials provide a light and reflective exterior and the south façade displays patterns of Arab geometry with photoelectric cells and mobile apertures allowing natural light control. It houses a museum, library, bookshop, cinema, restaurant and events spaces and hosts some fabulous events.

Musée National du Moyen Age (Musée de Cluny)

28 rue du Sommerard, 75005
+33 1 53 73 78 00
www.musee-moyenage.fr

The National Museum of the Middle Ages is one of the oldest sites in Paris, partly

built on the 'Thermes de Cluny': Gallo-Roman baths from the third century, with a frigidarium ('cooling' room) and gymnasium. In 1334, the abbots of Cluny resided here before being rebuilt in 1485–1510 by Jacques d'Amboise. In 1833 it was home to Alexandre du Sommerard and opened as a museum in 1843. It's a must visit for its Roman relics and collection of medieval treasures (jewellery, stained-glass windows, sculptures and, the pièce de resistance – the 'Lady and the Unicorn' tapestry series).

Musée du Luxembourg

19 rue de Vaugirard, 75006
+33 1 40 13 62 00
www.museeduluxembourg.fr

The neo-classical Musée du Luxembourg was built from 1884 to 1886 as an orangery in the north west of the Luxembourg gardens and held the first Impressionist exhibition in a national museum with works by Pissarro, Manet, Cézanne, Sisley, Monet and Renoir. Architect Shigeru Ban redesigned the space to add an Angelina teahouse and educational workshops.

Musée Rodin

77 rue de Varenne, 75007
+33 (0)1 44 18 6110
www.musee-rodin.fr/en

Hôtel Biron (originally Hôtel Peyrenc de Moras) was built between 1727 and 1732. The château-like house was the talk of the *quartier,* with its rococo-styled

Musée Rodin.

carvings, pavilions and approx. 3 ha. (7.3 acres) of grounds. Since 1919, it's been one of Paris' beloved studio-museums housing the works of once resident, the prolific sculpture Auguste Rodin (and works of his protégé/lover Camille Claudel, as well as pieces from Renoir's own collection, including artwork by Renoir and Van Gogh). The rosebushes sculpture garden is gorgeous.

Musée du quai Branly

37 quai Branly, 75007
+33 1 56 61 70 00
www.quaibranly.fr/en

In 1996, in the tradition of grand presidential cultural projects, President Jacques Chirac commissioned the Musée du quai Branly. Jean Nouvel created a fascinating urban hopscotch of shapes, colours and materials surrounded by a dense garden by the Seine. A monumental artwork by Aboriginal Australian artist Lena Nyadbi, based on her painting 'Dayiwul Lirlmim' (Barramundi Scales) decorates the roof and can be admired by those climbing the nearby Eiffel Tower. Discover the building by taking an architecture tour (check their site for details) then discover works that illustrate the richness and cultural diversity of the non-European civilisations from the Neolithic period to the twenty-first century. Stay for dinner at Les Ombres for its French cuisine and Eiffel Tower view (**www.lesombres-restaurant.com**).

Musée d'Orsay

1 rue de la Légion d'Honneur, 75007
+33 (0)1 40 49 48 14
www.musee-orsay.fr/en

The Musée d'Orsay was transformed into a nineteenth-century art museum from a defunct central train station: the Gare d'Orsay. Its Art Nouveau architecture sits majestically alongside the Seine. Lovers of Impressionism will be in heaven here.

Musée Maillol

59-61 rue de Grenelle, 75007
+33 (0) 1 42 22 59 58
www.museemaillol.com

This seventeenth-century rococo mansion sure has history. It was originally a convent, then became home to poet and novelist Alfred de Musset (1824–1840), was studio to painter Paul Baudry, became a cabaret (1951 and in 1955) and was finally bought by Dina Vierny, model of sculptor Aristide Maillol to collect and display the works of the artist. The museum exhibits Maillol's vast array of works alongside Vierny's private collection (including Rodin, Picasso, Degas, Rousseau and Duchamp).

Musée Cernuschi

7 avenue Vélasquez, 75008
+33 (0)1 53 96 21 50
www.cernuschi.paris.fr

After returning from a trip to Asia, Henri Cernuschi had this neo-classical mansion built by Dutch-born architect William Bouwens van der

Boijen, who was inspired by the current Italian tastes. The façade features mosaic medallions of Aristotle and Leonardo da Vinci. Bearded male sculptures (atlantes) support the wide cornice. High ceilings create a sense of serenity. After appreciating the majesty of the house and the collection of ancient bronzes, buddhas and sculptures, take a stroll in the romantic Parc Monceau.

Grand Palais

3 avenue du Général Eisenhower, 75008
+33 (0)1 44 13 17 17
www.grandpalais.fr/en

This huge exhibition complex built for the 1900 World Fair, and overseen by Charles Girault, covers an impressive 72,000 square metres (775,000 square feet) and is comprised of three major

Grand Palais.

Petit Palais.

sections: the Galeries Nationales, the Palais de la Découverte, and the Nave.

The building is architecturally unique, combining classicism, neo-baroque, Modernism and Art Nouveau styles. It boasts a dramatic, stone Beaux-Arts façade with palatial columns, and friezes. Art Nouveau elements include a massive glass roof, decorated with bronze statues of chariots and flying horses and a central horse shoe staircase with tree-like supports, mosaic floors and decorated iron balustrades. The imposing height and breadth of the building is a major factor of its modern brilliance, made possible by innovative techniques of the time which used reinforced concrete and iron.

Today it holds major art salons such as the FIAC (the International Contemporary Art Fair) and Paris Photo.

Petit Palais

Avenue Winston Churchill, 75008
+33 (0)1 53 43 40 00
www.petitpalais.paris.fr/en

Also built for the 1900 World Fair, this refined Beaux-Arts building has beautiful interiors with dramatic, high ceilings decorated with allegorical paintings. The fine art museum inside includes a terrific free permanent collection and a pretty inner courtyard café.

Musée Nissim de Camondo Hôtel Camondo

63 rue de Monceau, 75008
+33 (0) 1 53 89 06 50
www.lesartsdecoratifs.fr/en/museums/ musee-nissim-de-camondo

This elegant house, modelled on the Petit Trianon in Versailles, was offered to the state by Jewish banker Count Moïse de Camondo and named after his son Nissim, a pilot killed in the First World War. Scrutinise the chandeliers, silver dining sets, Beauvais tapestries, Chinese vases and needlepoint chairs, then glide through the library, the dining room, the private apartments and out to the garden.

Musée Jacquemart-André

158 Boulevard Haussmann, 75008
+33 (0)1 45 62 11 59
www.musee-jacquemart-andre.com/en

Once home to art collectors Nélie Jacquemart and Édouard André, this mansion houses many surprises from Rembrandt to Uccello to Canaletto. The elegant house has various salons, libraries and music rooms. Sip tea under the ceiling decorations by Giovanni Battista Tiepolo.

Musée Jacquemart-André. C Recourac

Musée de la Vie Romantique

16 rue Chaptal, 75009
+33 (0)1 55 31 95 67
www.vie-romantique.paris.fr/en

This lovely little free museum located at the foot of Montmartre was once home to Dutch painter Ary Scheffer and writer Amantine Lucile Aurore Dupin (nom de plume: George Sand) it was something of a society house with party guests including Dickens, Chopin and Delacroix. The 1830 *hôtel particulier* has a greenhouse, a paved courtyard and a

quaint garden (now with a café run by Rose Bakery). Come face to face with the royal Romantic portraits and admire the delicate furniture, as well as jewellery from the eighteenth and nineteenth centuries.

Musée Gustave Moreau

14 rue de la Rochefoucauld, 75009
+33 (0)1 48 74 38 50
http://en.musee-moreau.fr/

Gustave Moreau (1826–1898) was a prolific French Symbolist painter whose studio/house was constructed by his architect father Louis Moreau and is full of paintings and trinkets. In 1895, after inheriting the family home, Gustave called in architect Albert Lafon to extend the house and transform it into a museum. The spiral staircase is one of the main features today. Climb them to discover over 1,300 paintings, watercolours and sketches, and around 5,000 drawings.

La Cinématèque Française

51 rue de Bercy, 75012
+33 (0)1 71 19 33 33
www.cinematheque.fr

The national cinema archives and museum was inaugurated in 1996 as The American Centre. The deconstructive, asymmetrical building by Frank Gehry in the Bercy Park has something of a floating quality. Check the programme for the daily screenings of classics, themed programmes and new releases.

Cité de la Mode et du Design

34 quai d'Austerlitz, 75013
www.citemodedesign.fr

The Magasins Généraux were the first modern Parisian docks (designed by Georges Morin-Goustiaux in 1907 for the Port of Paris) to store merchandise on their way to the nearby Gare d'Austerlitz. The raw concrete (Brutalist) building was constructed from reinforced concrete and finished without decorative flourish – a Modernist concept that was both praised and criticised. In 2009, the building was re-inaugurated with a whole new function: a centre of design and fashion, the Cité de la Mode et du Design. The concrete structure was preserved with a 'plug over' of a new metal and glass fluorescent green snaky skin. At night the colours change (design by Yann Kersalé) and the rooftop becomes a trendy club 'Wanderlust'.

Musée National des Arts Asiatique Guimet/Galeries du Panthéon Bouddhique

6 Place d'Iéna/19 av d'Iéna 75016
www.guimet.fr/en

The Musée Guimet was built for Émile Guimet's prestigious art collection from Asia and Egypt. Inaugurated in 1898, its stand-out features include neo-classical columns, large rectangular windows and a rotunda. The museum is a haven of Asian arts spanning from Japan to Afghanistan, passing through China, Korea, Pakistan, Cambodia and India. The Panthéon Bouddhique is a wing of the museum, showcasing Japanese and Chinese art within a 1913-built *hôtel particulier*. A quaint wooden pavilion in the garden holds traditional tea ceremonies and is surrounded by a calming Japanese garden with bamboo, a lake and wooden bridges.

Louis Vuitton Foundation (2014)

8 avenue du Mahatma Gandhi, 75116
www.fondationlouisvuitton.fr/en

A total of 3,600 panels of curved glass create the twelve sails of this Frank Gehry-designed cultural centre. Inspired by late nineteenth-century glass and garden architecture and sitting in the Bois de Boulogne forest, the centre has been described as that of a giant iceberg, a cluster of clouds and a sailboat. 'To reflect our constantly changing world, we wanted to create a building that would evolve according to the time and the light in order to give the impression of something ephemeral and continuously changing' (Frank Gehry).

Much of the collection is site-specific and multi-media with international artists responding to the many interior and exterior spaces created by Gehry's architecture.

Fondation Pierre Bergé – Yves Saint Laurent

5 avenue Marceau, 75116
+33 (0)1 44 31 64 00
https://museeyslparis.com

Fashionistas will love this elegant *hôtel particulier* in the swish 16th

arrondissement that from 1974 to 2002 was the headquarters of the Yves Saint Laurent label.

Cité de l'Architecture et du Patrimoine

1 Place du Trocadéro et du 11 Novembre, 75116
+33 1 58 51 52 00
www.citedelarchitecture.fr

This museum dedicated to architecture and monumental sculpture is appropriately placed in the east wing

Cité de l'Architecture et du Patrimoine.
Ruby Boukabou

of the neo-classical Palais de Chaillot. Scrutinise replicas of important French monuments and hundreds of plaster casts from the twelfth century through to contemporary times. It's a dramatic exploration that begins and finishes with a front seat view of Paris' most famous monument of all: the Eiffel Tower! The permanent collection is also known as the Musée des Monuments Français.

Fondation Cartier pour l'Art Contemporain

261 boulevard Raspail, 75014
+33 (0)1 42 18 56 50
www.fondationcartier.com/en

The Cartier Foundation for Contemporary Art, designed by Jean Nouvel, creates a haven of peace and creativity off the busy boulevard Raspail. Six storeys of exhibition spaces and

Fondation Cartier pour l'Art Contemporain. Luc Boegly

offices are constructed in glass and steel and allow air and light. The surrounding foliage is particularly refreshing.

Palais de Tokyo

13 avenue du Président-Wilson, 75016
+33 (0)1 81 97 35 88
www.palaisdetokyo.com

Built for the 1937 World Fair (the International Exhibition of Arts and Technology), the Palais de Tokyo consists of two large wings connected by large colonnades. The east wing houses the Museum of Modern Art of the City of Paris and the western wing was transformed in 2001–2002 into a hip contemporary art gallery, the Palais de Tokyo. Stay for drinks or dinner at the chic Monsieur Bleu.

Musée Jean-Jacques Henner

43 avenue de Villiers, 75017
+33 (0)1 47 63 42 73
www.musee-henner.fr/en

Once home and studio of painter Guillaume Dubufe (1853–1909), this nineteenth-century mansion was opened in 1923 as a museum showcasing the artist's works which span Naturalism to Impressionism; historic to religious paintings. There's a grand piano for recitals and a lovely indoor winter garden.

Le Bal

6 Impasse de la Défense, 75018
+33 (0)1 44 70 75 50
www.le-bal.fr/en

Once a famous Roaring Twenties venue, Le Bal now produces exhibitions, publications and events centred around the contemporary image in the form of video, photography, film and new media. There are 300m^2 of exhibition space on two levels, a ground floor for installations (covered by an Art Deco glass canopy), a café, a bookshop and a garden with a glass-walled terrace for wind and noise protection.

Musée de Montmartre

8-14 rue Cortot, 75018
+33 (0)1 49 25 89 39
http://museedemontmartre.fr/en

In 1886 the Society of the History and Archaeology of Montmartre was founded to protect the thousands of artworks, sculptures and documents and in 1960 this lovely museum opened. The gardens have been renovated in line with Auguste Renoir's paintings. The artist was once resident here, as was Suzanne Valadon and her son Maurice Utrillo, Raol Dufy, and many other creatives. Kick back on a reconstructed swing from Renoir's 'La Balançoire' painting (1876 oil on canvas, now hanging in the Musée d'Orsay). Art of the bohemian Belle Époque is on the walls and wine wafts in the air thanks to the bordering vineyard. In the museum you'll discover the rural history of Montmartre, and original works from Toulouse-Lautrec, Modigliani, Kupka, Steinlen, Valadon, and Utrillo. Be transported into the studios, bars and cabaret of the Belle Époque; 'Le Bal du Moulin de la Galette' was one of the major Renoir works painted right here.

ENTERTAINMENT VENUES

PARISIANS ARE A cultured lot and people of all walks of life attend the hundreds of performances on offer nightly. Architects have been able to take some poetic licences while drawing on traditions to create venues in which people can gather to be entertained, and share cathartic experiences, through song, dance, comedy and drama.

Opera Houses
Palais Garnier

Place de l'Opéra, 75009
www.operadeparis.fr/en
Entry tickets purchased at entrance on rue Scribe

The 1875 Palais Garnier opera house is a declaration of love to the arts that

Palais Garnier.

Palais Garnier.

has stood the test of time. A creation of Charles Garnier, it was part of Napoleon III's great Paris makeover and constructed on top of a subterranean lake and a swamp. With Beaux-Arts symmetry and Baroque and Renaissance elements, the highly decorative opera employs marble, gilded bronze and has a concealed iron framework.

The exterior displays sculpted Greek deities, busts of famous composers, personified versions of Harmony and Poetry, monumental columns and glorious gilding. Interior highlights include the magnificent marble staircase, a velvet and gold auditorium (ceiling artwork by Marc Chagall) and long galleries with chandeliers and ceiling decorations of cherubs and clouds ... you'll float around and out on an operatic high, particularly when the sun is out as it creates a magical glow in the galleries.

Opéra Bastille

Place de la Bastille, 75012
www.operadeparis.fr

Inaugurated on the bicentennial of the storming of the Bastille, Paris' second opera house, (part of President Mitterrand's major works) is a stark

Opéra Bastille.

controversial proposal. The building has glass and granite walls, black upholstered seats and a large entrance staircase that dominates the place de la Bastille.

Theatres
Théâtre du Châtelet

2 rue Edouard Colonne, 75001
www.chatelet.com

This classical Palladian-style theatre with its symmetrical layout, columns and arcades was built by Gabriel Davioud under Baron Haussmann from 1860 and 1862.

contrast to Palais Garnier. The design competition was won by Uruguayan architect Carlos Ott with a modern and

Théâtre du Châtelet. Ruby Boukabou

Comédie-Française

1 Place Colette, 75001
www.comedie-francaise.fr

The national theatre was formed by Louis XIV in 1680, combining various local companies and is the oldest active theatre company in the world! Since 1799 they have been located in Victor Louis' regal Italian-style theatre, the Salle Richelieu, by the Palais-Royal. On display is a statue of Molière by Jean-Antoine Houdon as well as Molière's director's chair. Book well ahead for their weekend guided tours as they can sell out months in advance.

Théâtre de l'Opéra Comique

1 Place Boieldieu, 75002
www.opera-comique.com/en

Founded in 1714, this free-standing theatre by architect Jean-François Heurtier is a neo-baroque delight. Sadly, the original building burnt down in 1838 and again in 1887, but was rebuilt, and the one standing today was designed by Louis Bernier. This 'new' building used iron framework (typical of the Beaux-Arts style) in order to make it more fire resistant. The action takes place in the the Salle Favart named after the famous librettist Charles Simon Favart (1710–1792).

Théâtre de la Ville

2 Place du Châtelet, 75004
www.theatredelaville-paris.com/en

This neo-classical theatre opposite and mirroring the Châtelet theatre is now dedicated to dance. It has various outposts.

Odéon-Théâtre de l'Europe

Place de l'Odéon, 75006
www.theatre-odeon.eu

Close to the Luxembourg Gardens, the bold neo-classical Odeon Theatre was inaugurated by Marie-Antoinette in 1782. It was the first free-standing theatre in Paris and was also destroyed (twice!) by fire and the present building (in the neo-classical style) was opened in 1819.

Théâtre des Champs-Élysées

15 avenue Montaigne, 75008
www.theatrechampselysees.fr

Built in 1913, this was the first Art Deco building in the city. It was the first Paris theatre to be constructed with reinforced concrete (necessary for stability with its location close to the river). While classically inspired, the features are also stylised for a modern effect.

Théâtre du Rond-Point

2bis avenue Franklin Delano Roosevelt, 75008
www.theatredurondpoint.fr

Once Le Panorama National and later the 'Palais de Glace' (Ice Palace), this theatre, designed by Gabriel Davioud, is one of the Belle Époque prides of Paris with its circular form and dome roof. Once the place to go to see the works of Beckett and Ionesco, the Theatre du Rond-Point is now dedicated to staging the works of living playwrights.

Folies Bergère

32 rue Richer, 75009
www.foliesbergere.com/uk

This Art Deco icon (also featuring large Art Nouveau typography on its façade) was opened in 1868 as an opera house and modified to its current appearance in 1926. It became famous for its colourful revues with acts such as Josephine Baker dancing in her banana skirt.

Théâtre Édouard VII

10 Place Édouard VII, 75009
www.theatreedouard7.com

Built between 1911 and 1913 by British architect William Sprague, this theatre was the place to discover English plays. It's just around the corner from Palais Garnier, but tucked away from the hustle and bustle in a quiet little square. Enjoy a drink on the pavement in front of its neo-classical arches in the square that features a statue of King Edward VII.

Théâtre Mogador

25 rue de Mogador, 75009
www.theatremogador.com

This three-tiered English-style music hall was inaugurated in 1919 in the presence of US President Woodrow Wilson. It has produced operettas, Rolling Stones concerts, Molière award ceremonies and French versions of Broadway musical hits.

Théâtre de la Porte Saint-Martin

18 Boulevard Saint-Martin, 75010
www.portestmartin.com

An initiative of Marie-Antoinette, this beautiful theatre was built in just two months by architect Samson-Nicolas Lenoir (with round the clock workers) and opened on 26 October 1781 in the queen's presence. Later, it gained a reputation for high quality dramas by the likes of Alexandre Dumas, Victor Hugo and Honoré de Balzac. Burnt down during the Commune de Paris in 1871, it was rebuilt in 1873 by Oscar de la Chardonnière. The façade features sculptures by Jacques-Hyacinthe Chevalier and the interiors include a magnificent chandelier, a voluptuous theatre and splendid stained-glass windows in the upper reception rooms.

Théâtre de la Renaissance

20 Boulevard Saint-Martin, 75010
www.theatredelarenaissance.com

This attractive Italian-style theatre by the Porte Saint-Martin was built by Charles de Lalande, the assistant of Charles Garnier, from 1872 to 1873.

Théâtre National de Chaillot

1 Place du Trocadéro, 75016
http://theatre-chaillot.fr/en

One of the most elegant theatres in Paris, the large Art Deco Théâtre de Chaillot in the monumental neo-classical Palais de Chaillot, was built for the 1937 World Fair. It hosts French and international contemporary dance and theatrical productions as well as some fashion shows. Built on a hill, the innovative design by Jacques Carlu, Louis-Hippolyte Boileau and Léon Azéma, creates interesting perspectives as the foyers, galleries and entrances overlap. Be wowed by views of the fountains of Trocadéro, the Eiffel Tower and the Champs de Mars.

Théâtre des Abbesses

31 rue des Abbesses, 75018
www.theatredelaville-paris.com/en

This neo-classical/postmodern theatre

in Montmartre was designed by Belgian architect Charles Vandenhove in 1992 and opened in 1996.

Moulin Rouge

82 Boulevard de Clichy, 75018
www.moulinrouge.fr

The large (fake) red windmill was a beacon for punters to come and let down their hair at the Moulin Rouge cabaret (literally the 'red windmill'), founded in 1889 by entrepreneurs Charles Zidler and Joseph Oller. It helped people to brighten up after the dismal end of the Franco–

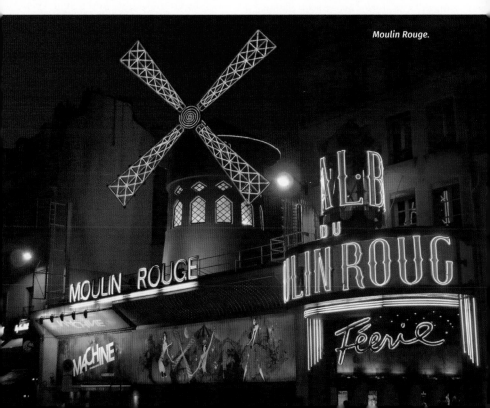

Moulin Rouge.

Prussian war. The original building burnt down in 1915 but was reconstructed and today is one Paris' major tourist attractions for glitzy traditional French cabaret revues starring the famous French can-can dance.

Circus-Style Tents

Cabaret Sauvage

59 boulevard Macdonald, 75019
www.cabaretsauvage.com

The wooden dance-floor, carved pillars, mirrors, booths and impressive lighting rig in this Spiegeltent circus tent in the Parc de la Villette make attending any concert, cabaret or event here a magical experience.

Cirque d'Hiver

110 rue Amelot, 75011
www.cirquedhiver.com/en

Circus, fashion shows, concerts and even Turkish wrestling competitions take place in this large 5,900 seat circus venue, opened by Napoleon III in 1852. Flying trapeze first wowed the world here, performed by Jules Léotard from Toulouse.

Concert Halls

Parisians love live music. The venues range from prestigious piano recital halls to football stadiums to regular cafés, and so the architectural styles range dramatically. Here are some of the more popular venues that will delight both your eyes and your ears. The best gig guide is Lylo (**www.lylo.fr**).

Salle Gaveau

45 rue la Boétie, 75008
www.sallegaveau.com

Prestigious piano recitals and chamber music performances are held in the former headquarters of the piano brand; an elegant turn of the century building (completed 1906) designed by Parisian architect Jacques Hermant.

L'Olympia

28 boulevard des Capucines, 75009
www.olympiahall.com

This mythic concert hall was opened in 1888 by Charles Zidler and Joseph Oller who, onto a good thing, next opened the Moulin Rouge. The façade is all about the billing – huge red lettering announcing the artists beneath the large Olympia signage. Edith Piaf, Charles Aznavour, the Beatles and Jeff Buckley are among the many stars that have all performed here.

Point Éphémère

200 quai de Valmy, 75010

This 1400m^2 space, once used to house construction materials, is now a trendy venue for concerts, rehearsals and exhibitions with a bar that spills out to the canal. It was set up in 2004 by Usines Éphémères, who have successfully transformed abandoned buildings into artistic spaces including Hôpital Éphémère and Mains d'OEuvres, in Saint-Ouen. The fire brigade is housed in the same quarters so occasional sirens punctuate the musical sets.

Bataclan

50 Boulevard Voltaire, 75011
www.bataclan.fr/en

The Bataclan (named after Offenbach's opéretta Ba-Ta-Clan) was designed by architect Charles Duval in 1864, inspired by a Chinese pagoda (originally called the Grand Café Chinois). The pagoda roof no longer exists and the former theatre and cinema now mostly hosts rock and pop concerts. The Bataclan was one of the locations of the 13 November 2015 terrorist attacks, with eighty-nine people killed and many others deeply traumatised. The faithful fans nonetheless soon returned to create new vibes at concerts with prominent and up and coming groups.

La Bellevilloise

19-21 rue Boyer, 75020
www.labellevilloise.com

In 1877, the four storey redbrick building in the heart of the 20th arrondissement housed a co-operative to help the less affluent access culture, education and political information and is considered a pioneer of the fair trade movement. Socialist Jean Jaurès held political gatherings here.

In 2005, a trio of agitators from the performing arts, Renaud Barillet, Fabrice Martinez, and Philippe Jupin reopened the space as an independent arts and entertainment complex for the public, business and the media, transforming the large building into various areas for concerts, screenings, parties, exhibitions and festivals. A café/bar with olive trees hosts musical brunches and a back terrace allows punters to take in the backdrop of hilly Ménilmontant while sipping mojitos.

Cité de la Musique

La Vilette
221 avenue Jean Jaurès, 75019

Also known as Philharmonie 2, the Cité de la Musique opened in 1995 and won Christian de Portzamparc the Pritzker Prize for his architecture. A bold work of contemporary architecture, the musical complex is comprised of concert halls, a museum, amphitheatre, library, rehearsal rooms and administration offices. Created as a 'dream-like town' in a shell-like form set behind glass, its passages, stairs, corners and halls play with light and perspective. New musicians admit to getting lost for the first couple of weeks of rehearsals!

La Cigale

120 boulevard de Rochechouart, 75018
www.lacigale.fr/en

Situated in Pigalle, La Cigale opened in 1887 as a café-concert venue before extending the programme to dance, comedy and music. In the 1980s, the interiors were brightened and dramatised by Philippe Starck.

Le Trianon

80 boulevard de Rochechouart, 75018
www.letrianon.fr/uk

This cult venue designed by architect Joseph Cassien-Bernard, opened in 1894 and restored in 2010, combines neo-classical Italian and Napoleon III styles and presents comedies, operas, revues and concerts. The opulent interiors encourage social flaunting.

Zénith Paris

211 avenue Jean Jaurès, 75019
www.le-zenith.com

This major concert venue was opened in 1984 and is one of the largest in Paris. Inspired by ancient Greek amphitheatres, it accommodates up to 9,000 people for popular entertainment in state-of-the-art technical conditions.

Philharmonie de Paris

221 avenue Jean Jaurès, 75019
https://philharmoniedeparis.fr

You can't miss Jean Nouvel's 2015 inaugurated Philharmonie when arriving from afar – it's reflective metal wings making it seem to be about to take off. The deconstructive structure in the Parc de la Villette is created with thousands of black, grey and white aluminium squares representing birds in flight. Nouvel employed hard and soft materials to create the sense of movement. Thick concrete walls block the noise of the surrounding traffic. The main auditorium was designed to create a sense of intimacy – the 2,400 seats are in an oyster-like shape so that no audience member is more than 32m from the conductor. For special occasions, like the Nuit Blanche, (an annual event where cultural establishments are open with events all night), you can visit the rooftop for a terrific view over Paris. Otherwise sign up for a guided tour on their site or visit one of its restaurants where you'll also get a good view of the park. (See also Cité de la Musique, page 133)

Studio de l'Ermitage

8 rue de l'Ermitage, 75020
www.studio-ermitage.com

World music and jazz concerts are of preference in this intimate music venue that was once a biscuit factory in the backstreets of Ménilmontant. The central stage and dance floor is overlooked by a mezzanine with tables and chairs. After the show, explore the area with its relaxed and lively bars, many also with free live music (they'll pass a hat for your tips- be generous if you like the music and they'll appreciate it!).

Stade de France

ZAC du Cornillon Nord, 93200, Saint-Denis
www.stadefrance.com

The national sports stadium also produces musical events from Carmen (opera) to Beyoncé. The elliptical shape of its €45 million roof symbolises the universality of sport in France and protects the audience from the elements while maintaining an open-air arena. The complex includes three galleries, twenty-two access bridges and many restaurants and shops.

Concerts also take place in bars all over Paris – classic bistro, jazz caves and small bars with people and tunes spilling into the streets, the music flavouring the air. The Caveau de la Huchette and the Caveau des Oubliettes are popular jazz cellars in the latin quarter worth checking out.

Cinemas

Parisians are film buffs and have access to many large and boutique cinemas to enjoy classic, art house and newly released films. After all, it was in Paris where the first public movie screening took place at the Grand Café on 28 December 1895.

Le Champo

51 rue des Écoles, 75005

Established in 1938 this art house

cinema was an old haunt of famous French film makers. The silhouette of Jacques Tati features on the faithfully renovated façade, just off the boulevard Saint-Germain.

Cinéma du Panthéon

13 rue Victor Cousin, 75005

The oldest surviving movie theatre in Paris dating back to 1907, the Cinéma du Panthéon, became the place to go for French new wave cinema. A salon/ tea room was designed by Catherine Deneuve to celebrate the establishment's 100th anniversary in 2007.

Action Christine

4 rue Christine, 75006

Catch a restored classic here and you're likely to be able to witness the architecture of Paris past. Opened in

Ruby Boukabou

Ruby Boukabou

1973 it's hidden away under the stone arches of an apartment block in the Latin Quarter.

Gaumont Opéra

2 boulevard des Capucines, 75009

Gaumont has various large cinemas around Paris. The neo-classic style entrance on boulevard des Capucines in the opera district is appropriately grand for its many film premieres.

Le Louxor

170 boulevard de Magenta, 75010
www.cinemalouxor.fr

Built in 1921 and renovated in the 1970s, the Luxor cinema opposite Barbès Métro station has Egyptian-themed decorative motifs of irises, papyrus and lotus flowers.

MK2

Quai de la Loire & quai de Seine
https://mk2films.com/en/

There are several MK2 cinemas around town where you're sure to find foreign films with subtitles instead of voice dubbing (hearing Leonard DiCaprio 'fluent' in French may be comic for five minutes but can be irritating, even if you are bilingual). Two of the most delightful locations are quai de la Loire and quai de Seine that sit opposite on each site of the Canal de l'Ourcq. The fluorescent blue, pink and red lighting reflect magically on the water and you can cross the canal on a small ferry between the two if you have a ticket.

Fondation Jérôme Seydoux-Pathé

73 avenue des Gobelins, 75013
http://fondation-jeromeseydoux-pathe.com

This contemporary wonder by Renzo Piano sits in thrilling contrast behind an Auguste Rodin sculpted façade (circa 1869). The five-storey building dedicated to cinema is covered with 5,000 protective shutters and raised over an internal garden. Luminous materials and a glass roof make the building shine and seem to float. Interiors are of wood and steel and the complex includes a screening room (often dedicated to silent films), film-themed exhibition rooms, collections of vintage cameras, Pathé archives and an airy research centre.

Studio 28

10 rue Tholozé, 75018
www.cinema-studio28.fr

Paris' original avant-garde cinema began life as a cabaret, opened in 1928. The floor of the entrance façade is painted red, a wink of a red carpet entrance and, oh, the candelabras just happened to be designed by Jean Cocteau.

La Cinématèque Française

(See page 121)

CIVIC & POLITICAL

Palais-Royal

8 rue de Montpensier, 75001
http://www.domaine-palais-royal.fr/en/

Built from 1629 as the private *hôtel particulier* of Cardinal Richelieu, the chief minister of Louis XIII, in order to be close to the Louvre Palace, the Palais-Royal (originally Palais-Cardinal) is a stunning neo-classical building complex. Although located in the centre of Paris, it is tucked away from the hustle and bustle of the streets.

Richelieu left the palace to the king and after Louis died, his widow, Anne of Austria, moved in with her young son, the future Louis XIV. Anne preferred this building to the large, cold Louvre palace as the courtyard enjoyed shelter from the wind and was (and still is!) a prime position for enjoying the sunshine.

Next, the notorious brother of Louis XIII, the Duc d'Orléans, took over and employed architect Victor Louis to rebuild the structures around the palace to create a commercial complex with galleries and boutiques that offered salons, theatres, shops and cafés for all classes, still in a neo-classical style. This resulted in both sophisticated dialogues and debates and late night debauchery (as a 'private' residence, the police couldn't interfere with the gambling and prostitution).

Today you can enjoy a quiet stroll under the elegant colonnaded galleries lined with upmarket boutiques, take a peaceful moment in the rose garden with a book, or a indulge in a quick photo shoot in the forecourt (cour

Palais-Royal.

d'honneur) with conceptual artist Daniel Buren's fun, though originally controversial, 1986 'Les Deux Plateaux' installation - 280 black and white striped columns of various heights.

The royal apartments now house the State Council and the Ministry of Culture and are not open to the public. However, you can visit the courtyard and gardens (see page 50) or book in for a tour/attend a performance at the Comédie-Française theatre that was part of the complex (see page 129).

Conciergerie/Palais de Justice

10 boulevard du Palais, 75001
www.paris-conciergerie.fr/en

This medieval complex on the Île de la Cité was home to Roman Emperor Julian the Apostolate in the fourth century, then to King Clovis in the sixth century, continuing on for the other monarchs from the Merovingian dynasty. It reached its peak when Louis IX had Saint-Chapelle erected within the property c.1242 in early Gothic style. When Charles V moved to the Louvre in 1360, he set up a concierge (official keeper of the king's household) in the western area and in 1431 the Supreme Court of Justice. History pivoted during the Revolution when the lower-floor prison (installed in 1391) held nobles and royalty before their execution by guillotine – including Marie Antoinette. Today you can visit the dramatic, vaulted spaces, the medieval kitchens and the cells. There are also temporary exhibitions with themes of the building's

history. As for the façade – while the magnificent gilded Tour l'Horloge clock tower dates back from the Capetian palace, the medieval-styled features such as the round towers were not actually added until the nineteenth century. The Palais de Justice is all neo-classical with Corinthian columns and stone staircases, but the law courts moved in 2018 to a dramatically contrasting glass building on the edge of central Paris (see below).

Tribunal de grande instance de Paris

Parvis du tribunal de, 75017

Conceived by Renzo Piano and inaugurated in 2018, this sustainable building unites the services of the high court, the police court, the public prosecution service and the twenty Parisian regional courts. Pre-stressed concrete beams support the ten upper floors and divert the weight towards the core. The columns and statues of the old tribunal are replaced with a focus on natural luminosity – the 160m tower is created with three parallelepipeds and over 50,000m^2 of glass walls that reflect the sky and symbolise the intended transparency of justice. The aim was to create a building where people, often in a situation of stress while awaiting a judgment, would feel some hope and peace rather than feeling intimidated and oppressed. Suspended gardens on the terraces were added as spaces for people to meet or reflect over views of Montmartre and the Eiffel Tower.

Assemblée Nationale (Palais Bourbon & Hôtel de Lassay)

126 rue de l'Université, 75007
www.assemblee-nationale.fr
Guided tours on Saturday (during Assembly), open visits Monday – Saturday (during adjournments) – check website. Take identification and dress conservatively.

The Palais Bourbon and the Hôtel de Lassay were originally built as villas for Louis XIV's daughter and were completed in 1728. After the Revolution, the Seine-side building became home to the French Parliament (National Assembly), with a semicircular meeting chamber added. It's impossible to miss the bold, neo-classical complex by the Pont de la Concorde, with its striking Corinthian columns and elaborate portico that were added in 1806 to mirror the Madeleine church on the opposite side (see page 99).

Hôtel de Lassay is the smaller of the villas situated on the west side of the Palais Bourbon and serves as the residence of the president of the National Assembly.

Palais de l'Élysée

55 rue du Faubourg Saint-Honoré, 75008
Visits of the gardens is possible during European Heritage Days.

The Élysée Palace was built from 1718 to 1722 as a Baroque-style palace and has been home to the President of the French Republic since 1873. The large corps de logis is framed by side pavilions, and a prominent Romanesque entry arch surrounded by four fluted Ionic columns.

Espace Niemeyer

2 place du Colonel Fabien, 75019

If you're venturing out of Colonel Fabien Métro station and wondering what on earth the wavy reflective glass building is alongside a giant goose egg-shaped object popping out of the ground … it's the 1980 work of Paris based modern/avant garde Brazilian architect Oscar Niemeyer to serve as the base for the French Communist Party.

UNESCO Headquarters

7 place de Fontenoy 75007
https://en.unesco.org

The seven-storey United Nations Education, Scientific and Cultural Organisation headquarters was a collaboration of international architects: Marcle Bruer (United States), Pier Luigi Nervi (Italy) and Bernard Zehrfuss (France), and approved by a prestigious panel of architects: Lucio Costa (Brazil), Walter Gropius (United States), Charles Le Corbusier (France), Sven Markelius (Sweden) and Ernesto Rogers (Italy). It was built with exposed, reinforced concrete in 'International Style', with a unique Y-shape with a curved canopy, and was inaugurated in 1958. Public events here include concerts and exhibitions (listed on their site) and their bookshop/gift shop is open Monday–Friday. Many great artworks hang in the building by the likes of Pablo Picasso, Joan Miró, Alexander Calder, and Alberto Giacometti.

Town Halls

The major and local town halls in Paris are not just administrative but also cultural, regularly hosting exhibitions relating to the city. Within and without, their architecture is often gobsmacking.

Hôtel de Ville

Place de l'Hôtel de Ville, 75004

Hôtel de Ville.
Ruby Boukabou

Paris' municipal government has met on this Right Bank site in central Paris since 1357! From 1553-1628 an elaborate Renaissance city hall was built. In 1871, during the Paris Commune, it was burnt down but another quickly erected inside the original stone shell (by architects Edouard Deperthes and Théodore Ballu), maintaining the Renaissance style but replacing royal symbols with republican declarations, such as the inscription of French national motto 'liberté, egalité, fraternité'. The masterpiece has ornate exteriors with sculptures and is surrounded with lamp posts and fountains. An equestrian statue of Etienne Marcel by Antonin Idrac was erected in 1888 on the Seine side of the building. Inside there are life sized nude statues, an elaborate staircase that parts and reunites and a function room in the style of Versailles' Hall of Mirrors with gilded carvings and decorative, vaulted ceilings. This is where, in 1870, the Third Republic was proclaimed.

Regular temporary exhibitions themed around the city of Paris are open to the public for free. The Paris Tourism Office is situated on the rue de Rivoli side.

Other town halls ('mairies') with impressive architecture include the town hall of the 1st arrondissement (4 Place du Louvre) with its neo-gothic façade and decorative neo-classical marriage chamber. In the 10th arrondissement, the Beaux-Arts-styled town hall (72 rue du Faubourg Saint-Martin) by architect Eugène Rouyer (built 1889-1896) boasts a sweeping central staircase. Prominent columns and pilasters with statues represent people of various local trades.

READING & EDUCATION

La Sorbonne

47 rue des Écoles, 75005
+33 (0) 1 40 46 23 39
www.sorbonne-universite.fr
Guided tours: visites.sorbonne@ac-paris.fr

One of Europe's most famous and oldest universities, the Sorbonne was founded in 1257 by Robert de Sorbon, chaplain and confessor to Louis IX. Its curriculum covered law, medicine, theology and the arts. Since 1821 it has been controlled by the Paris Academy and the École de Chartres, training students of archival conservation and preserving written heritage. In 1885 former Minister of Education Jules Ferrer authorised architect Henri-Paul Nenot to give the university complex an eclectic façade. The task was to harmoniously combine neo-renaissance, classical and antique styles. It was completed in 1901. The 1968 protests arose from here on 2 May and peacefully resolved on 29 May, succeeding as a social and cultural revolution, not a political one. The Sorbonne is now composed of four autonomous universities.

Libraries

Beautiful architecture of course helps inspire reading and writing. The current Bibliothèque Nationale de France (national library) building was one of Mitterrand's *grands projets*. Its construction from 1989 to 1995 was

Bibliothèque Nationale de France.

controversial for its costs (€254 million) and technical hiccoughs. But Dominique Perrault's postmodern construction really does have a charm. An inner sunken forest of three-storey high trees provides pleasant views for researchers and four glass towers are cleverly shaped like open books, reflecting in themselves.

At the Bibliothèque Publique d'Information (Centre Pompidou, rue Beaubourg, 75004) you can research under the modern industrial structures of the famous Pompidou Centre. The library hosts tours, debates, screenings and conferences.

The stunning Bibliothèque Richelieu (58 rue de Richelieu, 75002) designed by Henri Labrouste for Napoleon III (built 1859–1873) is a classical celebration of iron, with nine iron domes, glazed pottery and glass ceilings allowing natural lighting. As well as books, the library stocks prints, photographs, stage music, letters and antiques.

The imposing Bibliothèque Sainte-Geneviève (8 Place du Panthéon, 75005) in Romanesque and Beaux-Arts styles was an earlier work of Henri Labrouste (built 1838–1850) with carved stone exterior and large, airy reading rooms with neo-classical arches, modern iron barrel vaults and exposed iron columns. It was the first building to be purpose built as a library.

FINANCE AND BUSINESS

PARIS CERTAINLY HAS some flash banks: the royal-looking 1876–78 **Crédit Lyonnais** (17–23 boulevard des Italiens, 75002) with a façade imitating the Louvre's Pavillion de l'Horloge and a pediment depicting the distribution of loans; the 1878–82 **Banque National de Paris** (14–20 rue Bergère, 75009) with three neo-classical arches topped with statues representing Industry, Trade and Reason, while the 1906–12 **Société Generale** (29 boulevard Haussmann, 75009), is considered one of the most beautiful banks in the world with its magnificent stained opal glass dome and mosaic floors.

Billionaire businessman Francois-Henri Pinault (actress Selma Hayak's husband) has converted the nineteenth-century **bourse de commerce (stock exchange)** into an art museum with a team led by architect Tadao Ando. Opened in spring 2021 it features both temporary exhibitions from Pinault's private collection and other loans. The existing listed dome has been restored and modified with a central cylinder inserted to form an exhibition space. (2 rue de Viarmes, 75001, **www. boursedecommerce.fr/en/**). Catherine de' Medici's Hôtel de Soissons, built in 1575 by Jean Bullant, once stood on this site (see page 64 for the remaining astrological observatory column), but the current building is a modification of a 1767 grain exchange that rather resembles a bull ring. A wooden dome was added in 1783, but burnt down in 1802. Architect François-Joseph Bélanger proposed an iron replacement instead of a stone one to mimic the Pantheon in Rome. It was finally approved and in 1811 a light iron roof meant that trading was no longer conducted in the open air.

In 1889 it was remodelled with the copper leaves replaced by glass. The rotunda shape and the sheer size of the building makes it a stand out building in Paris' centre.

The Origami office building (34-36 avenue de Friedland, 75008, close to the Arc de Triomphe) designed by Manuelle Gautrand was built in 2011. The main façade is mostly glass, partially covered with a second-skin of screen-printed marble pattern that has an origami effect, visible from both exterior and interior. The panels are composite, a film of marble mounted on a twin layer of glass. The building was designed to achieve HQE certification (High Environmental Quality).

The building earned Manuelle Gautrand the 2017 European Prize for architecture. The award recognises European architects who have made a commitment to advance 'the principles of European humanism and the art of architecture'.

UNDERGROUND PARIS

PARIS ISN'T JUST about what's on the surface but also what lies, and lurks, beneath. There is, of course, the Métro, the practical underground transport where some stations also showcase art, but there's also the spooky catacombs, a sewers museum, an underground canal and caverns full of the good stuff – jazz, wine and cheese!

Le Métro

http://metro.paris/en/

In such a compact city, the Paris Métro is one of the most practical and popular ways to get around town (although locals are also embracing the public electric scooters and pushbikes). There are over 300 stations with many more being created as line extensions.

Civil engineer Fulgence Bienvenüe was the 'father of the Métro', with Line 1 inaugurated during the World Fair in 1900 and the rest of the original nine lines mostly completed by 1930. Extensions have been made ever since, with fourteen colour-coded lines, many of them being extended to Greater Paris. Escalators were introduced from 1909, and now service most stations – but often only ascending (inconvenient!). Most stations are only around 500m apart (convenient!). While most are underground, some stations are situated above ground on viaducts.

While the stations are relatively standardised, some have stand-out features including:

Cité (Line 4)

A throwback to the Art Nouveau style with round globe lighting and high arched ceilings.

Abbesses (Line 12)

The Hôtel de Ville Art Nouveau entrance moved here in 1974. Scenes of the historic countryside of Montmartre decorate the staircase (though it's the deepest station in Paris at 36m so be warned! There are also lifts/elevators').

Châtelet (Lines 1, 4, 7, 11 and 14)

This central Métro station is a rabbit warren of connecting corridors. The many entrances include a replica of an original Art Nouveau kiosk entrance, constructed in 2000.

Louvre-Rivoli (Line 1)

Opened in 1900 this station has replica

Egyptian and international artworks in glass cases set against marble walls to remind you where you are!

Concorde (Lines 1, 8 & 12)

Françoise Schein's tiled walls are like a word game. Installed in 1989 to commemorate the 200th anniversary of the French Revolution, the letters reassemble the Declaration of the Rights of Man of 1789.

Arts et Métiers (Lines 3 & 11)

The interiors resemble a submarine with round portholes and rounded copper walls.

Bastille (Lines 1, 5 & 8)

Tiled walls feature colourful depictions of the storming of the Bastille, local historic scenes and people (by artists Liliane Belembert and Odile Jacquot).

Line 14

The newest and the first fully automatic line, constructed in 1998, travels from Saint-Lazare to Olympiades. The newer platforms are brighter with more space with clear tiles for the floors and higher ceilings.

Ghost Stations

There are a number of ghost stations

Ruby Boukabou

that were either never used or have been closed, many since 1939 when France entered the Second World War. While some have been abandoned, others have been repurposed as film and tv sets (Porte des Lilas station, as seen in the film *Amélie*), homeless day shelters (Saint-Martin ghost station, situated between Strasbourg-Saint-Denis and République,) and even a cocktail bar (Croix Rouge, once terminus of Line 10 in the Latin Quarter, closed since 1939). You can visit some of the ghost stations on Journées européennes du patrimoine (European Heritage Days) **https://journeesdupatrimoine.culture. gouv.fr/**.

Métro 2030

Métro 2030 is the name of the scheme to create a cleaner, more modern Métro by 2030. This includes LED lighting that uses 50 per cent less energy and over €5 million a year invested in refurbishing and modernisations.

Mines and Catacombs

http://catacombes.paris.fr/en

Two building materials that define Paris, gypsum and limestone, were exclusively mined from land beneath and surrounding the city. From as early as the thirteenth century, gypsum was mined under Paris. It is ideal for improving the workability of soil and for building plaster, hence the name 'Plaster of Paris'. More notable

is the iconic Lutetian limestone particular to this area that evokes Haussmann's Paris. Stone was reused from abandoned ruins and in the tenth century mines were dug horizontally into the sides of hills. As scaffolding developed, the mines spread deeper and further. In the thirteenth century the city was expanding and construction often took place on mined land, causing collapses. In 1777 renovations of the tunnels began. There was the enormous task of rediscovering and identifying the locations, which they did by engraving in the tunnels the names of the streets above.

The story of the catacombs is both creepy and fascinating: in the late eighteenth century the cemeteries were overflowing. A solution needed to be found quickly before disease spread. The answer was found under the plain of Montrouge, the former Tombe-Issoire quarries, which at the time was outside the city walls (now in the 14th arrondissement). The Saints-Innocents cemetery was excavated first between 1785 and 1787 – it had been used constantly for ten centuries! The bones were transported by night so as not to shock the public or the Church ... The site was renamed 'Paris Municipal Ossuary' in 1786 and nicknamed the 'Catacombs', which referenced the underground burial places under Rome. By 1809 the underground passages of the dead were opened as an attraction to be visited by appointment.

Today there are over 550,000 visitors yearly. There can be a bit of a queue, so avoid school holidays or peak times where possible – or take a book to while away the time and a coat as you'll be waiting outside. The 1.5km circuit, lined with skulls, will take around an hour.

NB: There are 243 steps. Only bags measuring less than 40x30cm are allowed and there's no coat check.

The Paris Sewers Museum

Musée des Egouts
93 quai d'Orsay, 75007

Learn the history of the sewers and the variety of machines used within them on a tour of the 500m underground passage – if you dare. Haussmann's, and engineer Eugène Belgrand's, modern sewer system transformed the city, making it much cleaner and less stinky. A tour will help you appreciate today's relatively clean city.

Tunnel under the Bastille

The Canal Saint-Martin that connects the Canal de l'Ourcq to the Seine includes a 2km underground passage where the boats were once pulled along by workers, since it was too small for horses. Gliding through can be somewhat thrilling, with the tunnel lit by the boat's lights and large overhead circular skylights in the brick roof. Take a boat ride (**canauxrama.com**).

Caveau des Oubliettes.

Jazz caves

Attend a concert in one of the city's famous jazz basements. Go swing dancing at Caveau de la Huchette (5 rue de la Huchette, 75005), get spooked by the past while warming up with some funk or afro jazz at Caveau des Oubliettes (52 rue Galande, 75005), or get chatting to a young saxophonist or ten at a jam session at 59 Riv' (59 rue de Rivoli, 75001).

Wine and cheese caves!

You can also have an enjoyable time underground while trying some of France's best wines and cheeses in a former royal wine cellar (Les Caves du Louvre, 52 rue de l'Arbre Sec, 75001 www. cavesdulouvre.com). Get tips from the expert sommeliers while you sip and take in the ambiance.

PUBLIC PARKS & GREEN SPACES

PUBLIC PARKS AND gardens are necessary infrastructures in all populated cities. In 1991, under Jack Lang, President Mitterrand's Minister for Culture, an awareness of garden design, both heritage and contemporary, developed in governing bodies and has continued.

In September 2019 Paris had the highest population density in the European Union, with just under 11 million people in the whole city and just over 2 million inside the ring road, equating to 21,000 per km^2. Open, green spaces are essential for Parisians to re-oxygenate,

Tuileries Gardens.
Paris Tourist Office, Sarah Sergent

meet with friends and grab their doses of vitamin D! Real estate prices are high in the French capital, average apartment sizes are small and many children grow up without having a garden at home, meaning the parks become essential, offering Guignol puppet shows, sandpits, play equipment, merry-go-rounds and pony rides. There's also a lot of jogging, strolling, dog walking and picnicking happening. Columns, statues, bridges, kiosks, cafés, benches and lamp posts furnish the parks. Music festivals, open-air film screenings and exhibitions also take place here.

Here is a selection of beautiful parks that stay open all year long (under normal conditions), some until dusk and others 24 hours a day.

Jardins des Tuileries

Place de la Concorde, 75001

Stroll through the Tuileries in central Paris for a moment of serenity in the

city centre. In 1564 Queen Catherine Medici, widow of Henri II, commissioned Florentine landscape architect Bernard de Carnesse to create an Italian Renaissance garden. At 23ha (63 acres) it was the largest garden in Paris, compartmentalised with lawns, fruit trees, vineyards, and flowerbeds. Taking the name from the tile factories (tuileries) that were once there, the gardens glorified and glamorised the monarchy while providing them with some (ordered) nature.

In 1595 Catherine's son-in-law, Henri IV, was determined to rebuild and beautify Paris after the devastation of the thirty-year religious war. One of his projects was to restore and extend the gardens. He commissioned gardener Claude Mollet to create an ornamental lake, a fountain and plant mulberry trees for silkworms to support the silk industry.

In 1664 Louis XIV and his landscape architect André le Nôtre transformed the Tuileries into a formal French garden and opened up a central axis. In 1667 it was the first royal park to be opened to the public (except beggars and soldiers), before becoming a fully public park after the French Revolution.

Renovations in 1991–1996, aiming to recreate some of the gardens' former glory, were part of Mitterrand's *grands projets*. In 2013 another restoration programme was launched.

Pull up a chair by the lakes, admire the many replica statues, or grab a sandwich from a kiosk and snack by the flower beds. Then visit the Musée de l'Orangerie or the Galerie Nationale du Jeu de Paume, both located inside the gardens.

Jardin Nelson-Mandela

Passage de la Canopée – rues Rambuteau et Coquillère – rue de Viarmes – rue Berger – 75001

Opened in May 2018 in the centre of the new district of Les Halles, Nelson-Mandela garden offers a children's playground (7-11yrs), greenery, a misty mirror pond and an area housing ping-pong tables and sports courts.

Jardin du Palais-Royal

2 galerie de Montpensier, 75001

By the courtyard of the Palais-Royal sits this small, pleasant garden with benches, rose bushes and a statue of a snake charmer by Adolphe Martial Thabard (1875). Designed in 1633, the garden was transformed into a popular and remarkable floral haven in 1992.

Jardin des Plantes

57 rue Cuvier, 75005

Louis XIII's physicians' medical herb garden was created in 1626 as the Jardin du Roi (the King's garden), and by 1640 it was open to the public. Today there's plenty to do in these botanical gardens close to the Seine in the 5th arrondissement: visit the National Natural History Museum, play in the labyrinth, inhale the roses, step into the greenhouses and philosophise with an ancient tree.

Jardin du Luxembourg

Rue de Médicis – rue de Vaugirard, 75006

This sublime and peaceful park is situated in the heart of the Latin Quarter. In 1612 Queen Marie de Medici, widow of Henri IV, was inspired by the Boboli Gardens in her native Florence and commissioned Florentine hydraulics engineer and garden designer Tommaso Francini to create an Italian garden. In 1630 French garden designer Jacques Boyceau de la Barauderie transformed it into a more formal French garden. In 1811 neo-classical architect Jean Chalgrin (designer of the Arc de Triomphe) renovated the garden, preserving many of the features.

Covering 23 ha. (60 acres), it boasts an iconic octagonal lake with miniature sailing boats for kids, the Medici fountain, an Orangerie, the Pavilion Davioud, a rose garden, children's equipment, a bandstand and tennis courts. Joggers lap the outside paths.

Esplanade des Invalides

129 rue de Grenelle, 75007

Robert de Cotte, king's architect and urban planner, designed this lawn in 1704 to allow for war invalids to grow vegetables and mix with other Parisians.

Champ de Mars

2 allée Adrienne Lecouvreur, 75007

The Champ de Mars has been widely used: from a market garden to a military parade ground where Napoleon himself

Jardin du Luxembourg.

trained; from the site of Revolution protests to Bastille Day celebrations. This green area under the Eiffel Tower is now a popular place to relax or to picnic (tip – visit nearby market street rue Cler with delicatessens, cheesemongers, greengrocers, chocolate shops for goodies). There's a Guignol puppet show theatre for kids and several snack bars.

Parc Monceau

35 boulevard de Courcelles, 75008

This romantic park in the swish 8th arrondissement was designed by Louis Carmontelle, a set designer, painter, writer and landscape gardener, who was commissioned by the Duc de Chartes in 1778 to create a 'natural' garden. In 1781, Scottish botanist and gardener Thomas Blaikie re-landscaped parts of it. The concept was to have features representing 'all times and all places', which include a beautiful lake with Corinthian columns, a miniature pyramid and a rotunda. It was originally twice its current size.

Jardin des Champs-Élysées

10 avenue des Champs-Élysées, 75008

These large green spaces on either side of the Champs-Élysées were laid out by

Parc Monceau.
Ruby Boukabou

André Le Nôtre in 1667 for Louis XIV. In them you'll find the Grand Palais, the Petit Palais, Belle Époque pavilions, the Marcel Proust fountain, several elegant restaurants and a theatre.

In 1840 architect and archaeologist Jacques Ignace Hittorff beautified the garden after it had been used as a camping ground by foreign armies. It's a particularly pretty area to wander through in October amongst the falling autumn leaves.

Bois de Vincennes

Route de la Pyramide, 75012

In 1162 Louis VII built a hunting lodge in the ancient forest at the eastern end of Paris. With plenty of game, nature and fresh air, the site stayed a favourite for royalty and a château was constructed. It became a part-time residence for many generations from King Philippe-Auguste to Louis XV, who opened a semi-public park, having hundreds of trees planted to form alleys. From 1794 the grounds were used for military training. Then, under Napoleon III's regime, Haussmann appointed engineer Jean-Charles Adolphe Alphand as director of public works, who set about creating the modern, popular public park. He added features such as lakes, lawns, restaurants and even a hippodrome that would attract visitors and help pay for the park. Visit the zoo, the Temple de l'Amour ('temple of love'- see page 71), the flower gardens of the Parc Floral and the Château de Vincennes (see page 172).

Take a stroll, run, bike ride or even go rowing.

Parc de Bercy

128 quai de Bercy, 75012

Once a wine depot, this area was opened into a much appreciated green space in 1997 as part of French President François Mitterrand's *grands projets*. It holds a rose garden, fountains and playgrounds for children, lakes, ponds, large lawns and the Cinématèque Française (see page 121).

Parc Montsouris

2 rue Gazan, 75014

A lake, waterfalls, a Moorish pavilion and hilly paths are some of the features of this spacious park in the south of Paris that was built on a former limestone quarry. The park was created by Jean-Charles Adolphe Alphand, architect Gabriel Davioud and horticulturalist Jean-Pierre Barillet-Deschamps in 1867, in order to bring life to the abandoned quarter.

Parc André Citroën

2 rue Cauchy, 75015

Built on the site of a former Citroën car factory, the 14ha (34.5 acres) asymmetrical plot is divided into sections of lawns and themed gardens by the riverside. It was designed by a collaboration of architects headed by Alain Provest and is a meeting of the urban and the rural.

Jardins du Trocadéro

Place du Trocadéro et du 11 Novembre, 75016

The 10ha (24.71 acre) garden was created in 1878 by Adolphe Alphand then redesigned by Roger-Henri Expert for the 1937 World Fair to allow people to get up close and personal with the Eiffel Tower. Other features include the impressive Fountain of Warsaw and gilded bronze animal statues.

Bois de Boulogne

Bois de Boulogne, 75016

Originally known as Fôret de Rouvrey, this oak tree forest once stretched as far as Rouen. As the population grew, the forest was decimated despite efforts to limit the destruction. Birch was planted, but weeds invaded the depleted soil, while wars and climate caused further erosion. In 1750 Grand Master of Water and Forests, Nicolas Roneau, created the first managed forest, planting chestnuts and pines. In 1852 Napoleon donated the land to the city and in 1853 Haussmann hired engineer Jean-Charles Adolphe Alphand to design the park.

Today, there's plenty on offer in the 850 ha. (2100 acre) park on the western edge of Paris – horse riding, picnicking, rowing, jogging or just relaxing.... The Théâtre de Verdure is an open-air theatre here that produces concert and plays (including Shakespeare in French!) The Bagatelle gardens are beautiful with bridges, waterfalls, rocks, caves, a botanical garden, 10,000 rose bushes

and a nineteenth-century Chinese pagoda. Be warned, the woods by night are infamous for prostitution.

La Villette

211 avenue Jean Jaurès, 75019
https://en.lavillette.com

In 1977, French President Valéry Giscard d'Estaing decided to transform the former slaughterhouses at La Villette into a park. It was designed by architects Bernard Tschumi and Colin Fournier, after consultation with deconstructionist French philosopher Jacques Derrida.

Today it's a hub of cultural activity with not only the Cité des Science et de l'Industrie (Europe's largest science museum), but the Cité de la Musique (see page 133), the Philharmonie (see page 133), a jazz/world music bar, exhibition spaces, open-air cinema in summer, a Spiegeltent concert tent (see page 132) and a merry-go-round. On a pleasant day, stroll there along the canal from Jaurès (a leisurely half an hour).

Parc de Buttes-Chaumont

1 rue Botzaris, 75019

Once a Lutetian limestone quarry that gave Paris its definitive appeal (and also once its gallows!) the Buttes-Chaumont is now the pride of north east Paris and this writer's favourite place to jog, stroll, re-oxygenate and picnic (now open 24 hours in summer!). There are so many parts to explore including a lake, a rotunda lookout, a Guignol children's puppet theatre, a sandpit, bars and restaurants, a hot waffles and snack bar, a suspension bridge by Gustav Eiffel, a waterfall and caves. There's even Shetland pony rides for the kids.

Parc de Belleville

47 rue des Couronnes, 75020

Not far from the Buttes-Chaumont, the Belleville Park is a local treasure in the jumble of the cobblestone backstreets of this once working-class neighbourhood with a chequered history. Religious communities grew grapes from the Middle Ages (there are some vines there again) then in the nineteenth century it became a gypsum quarry. It's very steep and constructed of several layers with vines, lawns and flower beds. You'll also find a ping pong table, a rose garden and, best of all, an incredible Paris panorama from the top of rue Piat. Grab a table at Bistro Moncoeur opposite the top entrance to enjoy the view with a beverage (1 rue des Envierges, 75020).

Promenade Plantée, 'La Coulée Verte'

1 coulée verte René-Dumont, 75012

Take a walk along the 'floating' garden of Paris, a 4.6km (2.8 mi.) walkway along an old railway line from Bastille to Bois des Vincennes. The original line was built in 1859 and restored in 1988. Begin behind Opéra Bastille (on rue de Lyon, towards the crossroads with avenue Daumesnil) and allow a leisurely 1.5 hours to discover the 12th arrondissement from a whole fresh perspective perfumed with flowers and punctuated by birdsong.

Parc de Belleville.

Ruby Boukabou

Parc Rives de Seine

The central Paris Seine riverbanks have been turned into a nature friendly, sustainable zone, (the Right Bank from 2013 and the Left Bank from 2017). Jog, stroll, read and buy refreshments from the fair-trade outlets. You can even pedal on an exercise bike to recharge your phone!

Paris Plages – The Seine and the Bassin de la Villette

Going to the 'beach' in Paris may sound a little ridiculous, but in the height of summer this initiative has been embraced. Refresh under water sprays, kick back with an ice cream on a deck chair or go for a dip (if you dare!) in the Bassin de la Villette (from 6 July until 1 September).

English Squares, French 'Places'

As music is divided in sound and silence, cities are made of both buildings and open spaces. There are literally hundreds of squares in Paris, both green and paved, providing public spaces that break up dense areas. Some are dramatic, filled with monuments and surrounded by traffic, others are small and charming with terraced cafés where you can dunk croissants in hot coffees, toast champagne or bite into tasty croque monsieurs.

Be aware that the terminology can be a little confusing: a square (in English) is called a 'place' and what the French call a 'square' is a small green area of any shape, often with children's playground equipment and benches.

Square du Vert-Galant

15 place du Pont Neuf, 75001

Sit on a bench or under the willow tree in this picturesque location under Pont Neuf, between the two arms of the Seine. Considered one of Paris' most romantic spots, the triangular 'square' derives its name from Henri IV's nickname, the green gallant ('vert-galant'), as the king

Ruby Boukabou

was renowned for being a womaniser and for keeping many mistresses. Above the square, on the Pont Neuf, sits the 1818 bronze equestrian statue of Henri IV by Italian sculptor Pietro Tacca.

Square René-Viviani

25 quai de Montebello, 75005

This lovely, leafy, rose-scented garden,next to Shakespeare and Company bookshop, was actually once a graveyard. The central locust tree is said to be the oldest in Paris, planted in 1601. The square also contains old masonry from Notre-Dame.

Square Suzanne Buisson

7bis rue Girardon, 75018

Apart from the presence of the statue of the patron Saint of Paris, Saint Denis, everything about this quaint square in the backstreets of Montmartre will make you feel like you're in the south of France – from the large plane trees to the flowerbeds and petanque grounds.

Place du Châtelet, 75001

The Grand Châtalet building was demolished by Napoleon in 1802 and in its place was constructed a victory column and the Palmier fountain. Neoclassical theatres are on opposite sides.

Place Dauphine, 75001

Travel back to the seventeenth century in this refined triangular-shaped 'place' on the western end of the Île de la Cité, an early example of urban planning (1607) commissioned by Henri IV and named after the Dauphin (future Louis XIII). Situated on the west side of the Île de la Cité, off Point Neuf, its cobblestoned streets, the trees, the petanque games and the surrounding cafés add to the genteel ambiance. The rows of apartments with repetitive façades (though varied interior plans) resemble the Place Royale (now Place des Vosges) that was commissioned just before it, and was the first of its kind (see page 158). Shops and restaurants with terrace tables and awnings sit on the bottom floors and above are apartments topped with attics with domed windows. The third side faces the grandiose former Palais de Justice (see page 138).

Place de l'Opéra, 75002

The place de l'Opéra was created at the same time as the Opéra Garnier to help the public appreciate the new, magnificent opera house when passing by. Sip a café crème (café latte) at the swish Café de la Paix (5 place de l'Opéra) while marvelling at the opulence before you (see page 126).

Place de la République, 75003/10/11

This large square celebrates the Third Republic and serves as the meeting spot for many protests and rendez-vous. It's easy to get to with several

Métro lines running under it and easy to find with the monumental (9.5m/31ft) bronze statue of Marianne (the national personification of the French Republic, representing 'Liberty, Equality, Fraternity') holding an olive branch and the tablet of Humans Rights (by Léopold and Charles Morice, inaugurated 14 July 1883). Renovated in 2013, it's now the largest pedestrian square in Paris and the centre point between the Marais, the Grand Boulevards and the Belleville area. Skateboarders, street food stands and open-air Latin dances animate the square by day and night.

Place des Vosges, 75004

Built from 1605-1612 under Henri IV, Place Royale (now Place des Vosges) is the oldest planned square in Paris and a new model of plazas all over Europe. It is particularly stately with a large central fountain, manicured lawns, foliage and benches. Surrounding it are impressively symmetrical redbrick and stone buildings that sit majestically over arcades of cafés and boutiques.

Place de l'Hôtel de Ville, 75004

Dominated by the enormous Renaissance-style City Hall (see page 140) this square borders the Marais and the Seine and is beautified with magnificent multi-headed lamp posts and fountains, which provide convenient meeting points. Over the Christmas period, it transforms into a winter wonderland with decorations and a small ice-skating rink. There are plans to transform the place into an 'urban forest'.

Place des Vosges.

Fontaine Saint-Michel. Ruby Boukabou

Place Saint-Michel, 75005/6

Friends, dates and tour groups meet here under the grandiose wall fountain with the statue of Saint Michael slaying the dragon by Gabriel Davioud. Built in 1855 and enlarged by Baron Haussman, it sits just over the Seine from the Île de la Cité at the entrance of the Latin Quarter. Browse the surrounding bookshops or pop into Le Départ Saint-Michel – this bistro is open 24 hours so a 3am night cap or or 5am omelette is possible!

Place de la Contrescarpe, 75005

Situated in the Latin Quarter, this square was laid out in 1852 and is now the centre of a small roundabout with trees, a fountain, stone benches and lamp posts. Cyclists and scooter drivers pull up here to join friends at the bustling surrounding cafés that are particularly frequented by students and travellers.

Place de la Sorbonne, 75005

One of Europe's most famous universities can be enjoyed from this

Place de la Sorbonne. Ruby Boukabou

square with its fountains, trees and cafés, founded in 1639.

Place Saint-Sulpice, 75006

In front of the church of the same name, this large square features the monumental Fountain of the Four Bishops (Fontaine des Quatre Evêques) by Joachim Visconti, completed in 1848: four bishops sit facing each direction over protective crouched lions. Look out for the Morris Column and Wallace Fountain. When the chestnut trees are blossoming pink or the snow is falling, it's a particularly inspiring view. Soak it all up in the Café de la Mairie, popular with writers and students.

'Place' de Furstenberg, 75006

Although not technically a square, the five-globed lamp post and the Paulownia trees will likely inspire a gasp on first viewing. Try to pass by just after dusk as the lights flicker on. The surrounding florists, elegant apartments and the house of Eugène Delacroix (now a museum) add to the romantic vibes.

Place de la Concorde, 75008

The traffic around it may be a little wild,

but the Place de la Concorde is one of Paris' most handsome squares, situated between the Tuileries, the Seine and the Champs Elysées – and it has history! Designed by Ange-Jacques Gabriel as an octagon in the mid-eighteenth century and originally called place Louis XV, it was then transformed into the 'Place de la Revolution', where the public guillotine executed royals and nobility – including Louis XVI and Marie Antoinette. The pièce de résistance is the ancient 23m Luxor obelisk, a gift from Egypt in 1836 (see page 66). Two monumental fountains were added in 1840 by Jacques Ignace Hittorff. Rickshaw rides depart from here.

Place Saint-Georges, 75009

Step back in time into this beautiful little square in the Quartier de la Nouvelle Athènes and let out a sigh while passing the iconic red and white Métro sign, the lamp posts, the classic French café terrace and the cherry blossoms under Haussmann-style townhouses.

Place Charles de Gaulle, 75008/16/17

Formerly known as Place de l'Étoile, a total of twelve avenues designed by Baron Haussmann shoot out from the Arc de Triomphe (see page 68) to form a star shape (étoile). Traffic here is quite crazy, so make sure to use the underground tunnels. This is the top entrance of the Champs-Elysées and was renamed Place Charles de Gaulle after the former French President's death in 1970.

Place Pigalle, 75009

Once the centre of the impressionists' ateliers and the address of their favourite café, Place Pigalle later became renowned as the centre of the red-light district of Paris, with fluorescent signage on the boulevard of sex shops and seedy bars. However, it is changing and becoming an area of hip cocktail bars and cafés, particularly to the south, nicknamed 'So Pi'.

Place Sainte-Marthe, 75010

Grab a table on the terrace of La Sardine for tapas and wine or Perrier while appreciating this quaint and beautiful hidden pedestrian square in Belleville. Afterwards, stroll down the colourful rue St Marthe bursting with record shops, South American, Spanish and African restaurants.

Place de la Nation, 75011

A former guillotine site and starting point for many demonstrations, the central piece of this large square is the 1899 'Le Triomphe de la République' bronze statue by Aimé-Jules Dalou. Magnificent flower beds and typical French bistros surround the square.

Place de la Bastille, 75011

Where the infamous prison once stood, people now rush around shopping by day and meeting at night for opera or drinks and meals at the large terraced cafés. The Colonne de Juillet is brilliant and visible from afar (see page 65). The 3D Timescope terminal (located on the corner of boulevard Richard Lenoir) makes for a unique experience, plunging you back into 1446! **www.timescope.com**

Place d'Italie, 75013

Place d'Italie was renovated in 2019 to be more pedestrian friendly and green with a 'miroir d'eau' reflective pond and a large garden with Paulownias that flower in blue/mauve in the spring. Nonetheless, this is a major traffic intersection and if you really want to relax, it's a short walk to the Jardin des Plantes or the village-like Buttes-aux-Cailles area.

Place Paul Verlaine, 75013

Place Paul Verlaine resembles a village square in the Butte-aux-Cailles with a well, a fountain, benches and a petanque ground. Pack your swimming costume for a dip in the neighbouring Art Deco swimming pool (Piscine de la Butte-aux-Cailles)!

Place du Trocadéro, 75016

This is where you'll get your best photo of the Eiffel Tower. No surprises, you'll be joined by a throng of tourists and street vendors with their miniature Eiffel Towers and fluorescent shooting toy rockets (unless you arrive at sunrise). Nonetheless, the square oozes majesty, surrounded by the Palais de Chaillot with its sculpted Apollo and Hercules statues, hazel and walnut trees and gilded bronze statues.

Place du Trocadéro at sunrise.

Place du Tertre.

Place du Tertre, 75018

At 130m high, this square is the heart of touristic Montmartre and packed with terraced cafés and landscape and portrait painters. It's frenetic but beautiful and the quality of the light against the trees and café awnings will allow you to understand the artists' inspirations here. Pick up an original Paris landscape by a local artist or have your portrait sketched. Make sure to find Jean Jacques Duverger's gorgeous floral paintings.

Place des Abbesses, 75018

It's hard not to be charmed by this square, half way up the hill of Montmartre, with its original wrought iron Art Nouveau Métro entrance, pavements, surrounding bakery, Saint-Jean church and bistro.

Place de Ménilmontant, 75020

With its vibrant street art high up on the walls and popular cafés spilling out all around, this square is a busy multicultural crossroads. From here you can join the bustling fruit and veg markets along the boulevard (Tuesday and Friday mornings) or, by night, find dozens of affordable bars and restaurants, often with live music. Got a couscous craving? You're in the right spot!

Place des Grandes Rigoles, 75020

This lovely square on rue des Pyrénées is best appreciated over a café crème at the 3 Rigoles café opposite.

Place Gambetta, 75020

Place Gambetta was greened up in 2019. It is surrounded by buzzing bistros, florists and newspaper kiosks and a Renaissance-styled local town hall.

CEMETERIES & THE PANTHÉON

Cemeteries

Visiting the cemeteries in Paris is sometimes spooky, sometimes poetic and always fascinating. They provide places to reflect on life while paying homage to some of the famous artists, architects and people of Paris past. Discover busts, stained-glass windows, ornamental gates, sculptures, planters, reliefs, crosses and acroteria in Gothic, classical and contemporary designs.

Père Lachaise

8 boulevard de Ménilmontant, 75020

Stroll through this beautiful and famous cemetery in the 20th arrondissement, the most visited necropolis in the world, to visit classical and quirky tombs.

This first municipal cemetery in Paris was opened in 1804 and named after Father ('Père') François de la Chaise, who lived in the chapel on site and took Louis XI's confessions. Commissioned by Napoleon I, architect Alexandre-Théodore Brogniart designed an English garden-style cemetery featuring an abundance of greenery. The cemetery was not originally very popular until the transferral of the likes of Jean de La Fontaine and Molière made it trendier!

It worked and is now star studded. You can also pay your respects to Balzac, Chopin, Jim Morrison, Marcel Proust, Sarah Bernhardt, Marcel Marceau, Théodore Géricault, and Oscar Wilde (the sculpture on his tomb is by Jacob Epstein and is covered in lipstick kisses from fans). Wondering through the large hilly terrain is always a pensive, calming experience.

Montmartre

20 avenue Rachel, 75018

This pretty, shady cemetery opened in 1825 on the site of a former quarry. Look over the cemetery from the Pont Caulaincourt or enter to discover the classical, Gothic, Renaissance, neo-Egyptian and Art Nouveau-styled tombs under chestnut and maple trees. The grave of architect Jacques Ignace Hittorff is here: a member of the Académie of Beaux-Arts, his works included the cast iron and glass dome roof of the stock exchange under Bérange (see page 142), the church of St Vincent de Paul and the Cirque d'hiver (see page 132). Others highlights include the tombs of La Goulue (Louise Weber, the original French cancan-dancer of the Moulin Rouge); painters

Edgar Degas, Victor Brauner, Horace Vernet and Václav Brožík; Dalida and sculptor Aimé Morot.

Montparnasse

3 boulevard Edgar Quinet, 75014

Pay respects to Gabriel Davioud (1824–1881), inspector general for architectural works in Paris, and chief architect for its parks and public spaces under Haussmann. Then navigate various styles of tombstones while noting the many famous names including Jean-Paul Sartre, Simone de Beauvoir, Charles Baudelaire, Antoine Bourdelle, Constantin Brâncuși, Samuel Beckett and Man Ray! You'll also find a version of Romanian Modernist sculptor Constantin Brâncuși's 'The Kiss', and Horace Daillion's 'The Génie du Sommeil Eternel', a bronze angel of Eternal Sleep.

Passy

2 rue du Commandant Schloesing, 75016

Close to the Eiffel Tower in the well-do-do 16th arrondissement, this small but much visited cemetery, opened in 1820, houses the grave of architect Hector-Martin Lefuel (most famous for completing the Louvre following the death of architect Visconti in 1863), painter Edouard Manet, composer Claude Debussy, and former French President Alexandre Millerand, among others. The chestnut trees add a poetic touch.

The Panthéon

Place du Panthéon, 75005
+33 (0)1 44 32 18 00
www.paris-pantheon.fr/en

The Pantheon is the one of Paris' most glorious neo-classical buildings, inspired by Rome's Pantheon, London's St Paul's Cathedral and ancient Greek temples, particularly those visted in Paestum by architect Jacques-Germain Soufflot during his Italian travels. Perched on Montagne Sainte-Geneviève, the immense 83m (272ft) tall building was originally built as a church and was King Louis XV's way of thanking Saint Geneviève, the patron Saint of Paris, for his recovery from severe illness.

Massive stone columns support the iron reinforced grand portico, which

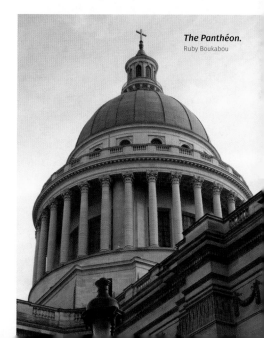

The Panthéon.
Ruby Boukabou

is decorated with a relic of Mother France presenting laurels to the great men of France, forming part of Jean-Baptiste Rondelet's transformation of the building from a place of worship into a prestigious mausoleum after the Revolution.

Inside, massive Greek columns are part of the ode to antiquity, the ground plan is a Greek cross and two small cupolas sit beneath the high dome, where a replica of Faucualt's pendulum dangles to dramatic effect. Massive, mesmerising murals depicting the life of Geneviève by Symbolist painter Puvis de Chavannes decorate the walls. On view in a small side room is a miniature model of the building for visitors to scrutinise the structure's design. Beneath is a sober, barrelled vault with tombs of the likes of Voltaire, Dumas, Rousseau, Zola and Hugo.

The Pantheon is a stop on the Arènes de Lutèce walking tour (see page 202). From April until October, for a few extra euros, it's possible to climb to the colonnade around the dome for tremendous views.

CHÂTEAUX

IT WOULD BE a shame to go all the way to France and not visit a château! Many of these former royal residences, homes to nobility, hunting lodges and aristocratic retreats are now open to the public with museums, variously themed guided tours and cultural activities for all ages. They are mostly located outside of central Paris, so set aside the best of a day if possible to ensure a relaxed visit with travel, queues, and extra time to explore the magnificent gardens and opulent decorations, surrounding villages and forests. Where possible, buy your tickets online in advance for a quicker and smoother entry.

Château de Versailles

Place d'Armes, 78000 Versailles
http://en.chateauversailles.fr

Versailles began life in 1623 as a modest brick and wood hunting lodge for Louis XIII. But the palace as we know it today was the project of the Sun King – Louis XIV, by architects Louis Le Vau and Jules Hardouin-Mansart, with Charles Le Brun overseeing interiors. The layout represents the structure of the kingdom with the king's bedroom at the centre as, like the sun, everything else revolved around his presence. The palace exhibits

Versailles Palace.

Italian-influenced French Baroque brilliance with painted vaults, columns, gilding and marble. The main attractions include the Hall of Mirrors, the Royal Opera, the Grand Trianon, Royal Apartments and Marie-Antoinette's Hamlet. The Petit Trianon, a small château, represents a more simple and elegant neo-classical style, completed by Ange-Jacques Gabriel. The gardens by André Le Nôtre are magnificent with flowers, fountains, marble basins, and statues in symmetrical French garden style. There are plenty of artistic events during the year including musical fountain shows and a decadent masked ball in summer.

Château de Saint-Germain-en-Laye

Place Charles de Gaulle, 78100 Saint-Germain-en-Laye
https://musee-archeologienationale.fr

Not far from Versailles is a magnificent French Gothic castle built in 1124 by Louis VI, extended in the 1230s by Louis IX, burnt down in 1346 by Edward of Woodstock (aka The Black Prince) and rebuilt by Charles V in 1360. But it was François I who oversaw the current palace from 1539, later extended in the French Renaissance style. The symmetrical Italian-style garden was also later transformed into the 'French' style gardens. Today it's the home of the National Archaeology Museum.

The château is easy to access by public transport, situated directly opposite Saint-Germain-en-Laye station. Before dashing back to Paris, visit the beautiful 1827 Saint-Germain-en-Laye church with its massive Tuscan columns, sculptures and artworks, then wander around the cobblestoned backstreets to enjoy the relaxed ambiance and quaint cafés and restaurants.

Château de Monte-Cristo

Chemin du hauts des Ormes, 78560 Le Port-Marly
www.chateau-monte-cristo.com/en

Alexandre Dumas, author of *The Three Musketeers* and *The Count of Monte-Cristo*, had this charming, small, Renaissance-style château built by architect Hippolyte Durand in 1846. The façade features carved flowers, angels and portraits of the likes of Shakespeare and Danté. *'J'aime qui m'aime'* (I love those who love me) is carved under the Dumas family coat of arms and the pinnacles of the two turrets are inscribed with the author's initials. The first floor has a Moorish-themed salon once used for entertaining. In the grounds is the small neo-gothic Château d'If, which served as his writing studio, its façades decorated with fictional heroes and carved titles of his works. Dumas fled to Belgium and then Russia to avoid creditors, but the estate was saved and restored. Today it's open for visits and hosts exhibitions and literary events.

Château de Monte-Cristo.

Château de Fontainebleau

77300 Fontainebleau
www.chateaudefontainebleau.fr

The palace of Fontainebleau was built from the twelfth to the nineteenth century as a royal residence (including the Valois, the Bourbons, Philippe d'Orléans and Napoleon III). Medieval features include the 1137 keep and the interior passageways and spiral staircases. François I added major developments after returning from Italy with Italian Renaissance artworks, designers and craftsmen. Of note is the finely decorated gallery connecting his chamber to the chapel. The famous horse shoe entrance staircase, reconstructed in the era of Louis XIII (by Jean Androuet du Cerceau), is one of its most significant features and a model of the Italian Renaissance style. The palace has over 1,500 rooms and 130ha. (321 acres) of French and English gardens and parks. Relax afterwards on the terrace of a café at place Napoleon, a few minutes' walk from the entrance.

Château de Fontainebleau.

Château de Vaux-le-Vicomte.

Château de Vaux-le-Vicomte

77950 Maincy
https://vaux-le-vicomte.com

This mid-seventeenth century Baroque masterpiece was originally the home of Nicolas Fouquet, Superintendent of Finances in France under Louis XIV. With his wealth and influence, Fouquet employed the top architects and artists of the day: the famous architect Louis Le Vau, landscape gardener André Le Nôtre and interior decorator Charles Le Brun. Sound familiar? It's the dream team that went on to work at Versailles for Louis XIV. The château has been privately owned since 1875 but is open to the public.

Château de Chantilly

Château de Chantilly, 60500 Chantilly
www.domainedechantilly.com/en

The Château de Chantilly with its wide moat and esplanade may be recognisable: it was the home of the James Bond villain Max Zorin (Chistopher Walken) in *A View to a Kill*.

Constructed on marshlands, the château went through various transformations from the Middle Ages to the nineteenth century. After several bloody French dramas, it became the centre of vibrant royal society with Le Nôtre stepping in to create the gardens. Henri d'Orléans, Duke of Aumale, a passionate collector of manuscripts

Château de Chantilly.

and artworks, left the estate to the Institut de France in 1897 and it was opened to the public as the Musée de Condé, boasting works by the likes of Delacroix, Poussin and Raphael. The Living Museum of the Horse in the Great Stables attracts many visitors and presents impressive equestrian shows throughout the year.

Château de Vincennes

Avenue de Paris, 94300 Vincennes
www.chateau-de-vincennes.fr/en

This fourteenth-century château on the eastern edge of Paris was originally built as a hunting lodge for Louis VII c.1150. The château became a royal residence and later a prison, where the infamous Marquis de Sade was held. The fortress has the highest dungeon in Europe, standing at over 50m high and visitors can climb the 250 stairs if keen. Guided tours by the Centre of National Monuments (Centre des Monuments Nationaux) are a great way to gain historic and architectural insights. Make sure to check their site for various events and concerts.

Château de Breteuil

78460 Choisel
www.breteuil.fr

Just 35km to the south west of Paris, overlooking the Chevreuse Valley, this French Baroque château hosts interpretations of French author Charles Perrault's fairy tales (*Little Red Riding Hood, Sleeping Beauty, Puss in Boots, Cinderella ...*). Wax sculptures, made by the Grevin museum, are on display. The building is thought to date back to the Gallo-Roman period. The fortified castle, with medieval square moats and a dovecote, is still owned by the de Breteuil family.

Château de Pierrefonds

Rue Viollet le Duc, 60350 Pierrefonds
www.chateau-pierrefonds.fr

Built by Louis d'Orléans, demolished by Louis XIII and rebuilt by Napoléon III, the château de Pierrefonds has passed through various styles throughout its life, although its stand-out features are its medieval towers, large fortress and ornate decorations. It seems like a setting for a fairy tale...

Château de Pierrefonds.

Pont Neuf.

BRIDGES

LES PONTS (BRIDGES) are quintessential to Paris. Few rivers in the world have as many spans across them as the Seine (thirty-seven in total), each with its own history, style and significance to Parisians. Below are some of the best, following the Seine upstream (west to east). To cross ten in one easy walk, flick to the Walking Tours section (see page 184)

Pont de Bir-Hakeim, 75015

Cars, pedestrians and trains share this bridge, a favourite location for films and clips with the Eiffel Tower looming in the background. The thin metal colonnades, hanging tear-drop lamps and decorations are from the first decade of the twentieth century, a period when industrialisation was a positive, even romantic, notion compared to the heavy

Pont de Bir-Hakeim.

nature of masonry. If you happen to be there at sunset when the lights of the bridge, and the Eiffel Tower flash on, your heart will skip a beat.

Passerelle Debilly, 75007

This is another example of the industrial era's use of steel, but is more minimalist in style as it was only built as a provisional bridge for foot traffic to the World's Fair in 1900. In 1941 it was deemed of little historic interest and threatened with

demolition. Luckily it survived and its simplicity is now its greatest charm.

Pont de l'Alma, 75008

Built in 1856 for Napoleon III to commemorate the Battle of Alma in the Crimean War, this bridge features statues including a French soldier (Zouave) that was once used to gauge the water level of the Seine. There's a wonderful view of the Eiffel Tower from here. The bridge is also famous as it is

Passerelle Debilly.

above the tunnel where Princess Diana died in a car crash.

Pont Alexandre III, 75008

This is an exquisite example of Art Nouveau elegance, built in 1900. It was the first to install electric lighting, using beautifully ornate candelabras. It also includes gilded statues of winged horses symbolising Arts, Sciences, Commerce and Industry. It is a favourite location for wedding photos and Instagrammers, with the Eiffel Tower in the background. Adele crosses the deserted bridge in the music video for *Someone Like You*. Oh, and you can party underneath it at Showcase nightclub.

Pont de la Concorde, 75001

Construction of this neo-classical bridge started in 1789 but was slowed down due to lack of building material. Serendipitously, the nearby Bastille came crashing down along with the monarchy, leaving a huge pile of ... stones! So, a notorious prison became a bridge. If you trust your balance and the time is right, jump up to sit on the stone walls to catch a golden pink sunset over the Eiffel Tower.

Passerelle Léopold-Sédard-Senghor, 75001

This footbridge connects the Musée d'Orsay to the Jardin des Tuileries, two of

Pont Alexandre III.

Paris' great attractions. It was designed by architect Marc Mimram in 1999, and won the prestigious architecture award 'Prix de l'Équerre d'Argent' that year. It is covered in Brazilian wood, has a single span and no piers, but is secured by hefty concrete pillars. It is named after Senegalese president, poet and writer Léopold Sédar Senghor (1906–2001).

Pont Royal, 75007

The third oldest bridge in Paris (after the Pont Neuf and the Pont Marie), this 100m (328ft) stone bridge with five arches was commissioned by Louis XIV and built between 1688 and 1689 by architect Jules Hardouin-Mansart.

Pont du Carrousel, 75007

Architect Antoine-Rémy Polonceau broke the norm on Paris bridges by designing an arch bridge instead of a suspension bridge for aesthetic reasons (no towers or cables to distract from the Paris skyline). Made from cast iron and timber,

the bridge, inaugurated in 1831, was later replaced by a sturdier structure with reinforced concrete, keeping some of the design qualities of the original.

Pont des Arts/Passerelle des Arts, 75006

This romantic footbridge connecting the Louvre (Right Bank) to the Institut de France (Left Bank) was one of the main victims to the lovelock (padlock) craze, a sort of mass vandalism and pollution (with the keys thrown into the Seine and the bridge sagging dangerously under the weight of all that heavy commitment). The original 1802 bridge was the first metal bridge in Paris, but was rebuilt in 1984 after a barge crashed into it. People have been known to have picnics, film videos, paint huge landscape paintings and propose marriage on this bridge, so be prepared to be inspired!

Pont Neuf, 75001

Despite its name, Pont Neuf (New

Pont au Change.

Bridge) was built in 1604 and is considered the oldest bridge in Paris. It was opened by Henri IV, whose statue on horseback graces the middle of the two spans. It crosses the Seine at the western tip of the Île de la Cité, connecting the Right and Left Banks. The bridge is Romanesque, with twelve stone arches in total, and has bastions designed for pedestrians to avoid muddy splashes from passing horses and carts. The foundations are decorated with 'mascarons' – grotesque stone carved figures meant to deter evil. It has a colourful and violent history of street vendors, entertainers, villains and slave merchants, which continues in a very mild form today with child scammers pretending to be deaf and dumb then picking pockets of tourists who sign their fake petitions. The bridge is captured in Auguste Renoir's masterpiece, Pont Neuf.

Pont au Change, 75001

This bridge crosses from the Conciergerie on the Île de la Cité to Place du Châtelet on the Right Bank. In the twelfth century it became a place for foreigners and traders to exchange currency. The current bridge was finished in 1860 under the reign of Napoleon III.

Petit Pont, 75005

This simple stone arch is the thirteenth bridge to occupy this site. The first was built by the Parisii, the Celtic tribe who lived on the Île de la Cité before the Romans arrived. The latest bridge is the sturdiest yet, consisting of one span and raised high to allow boats to easily pass underneath. Crossing it today gives you a feeling of connecting with more than 2,000 years of Paris history.

Pont au Double, 75004

This simple cast iron bridge contrasts

beautifully with the masonry to which it clings. It received its name from the toll paid by pedestrians who were originally charged a 'double' coin to cross it. A stone staircase leads down from the bridge to the banks of the Seine.

Pont de l'Archevêché, 75004

This quaint, narrow, three-arched stone bridge links the Île de la Cité to the 5th arrondissement, just behind Notre-Dame. It was built in 1828 and was another victim of the lovelock craze.

Pont Saint-Louis, 75005

From behind Notre-Dame you can wander over to the charming, village-like Île Saint-Louis via this pedestrian bridge, a favourite for buskers.

Pont Marie, 75004

Pont Marie, the second oldest bridge in Paris, took twenty years to build and was finished in 1635. It originally had houses built on it, but when a partial collapse in a flood in 1658 led to scores of deaths, the remaining houses were removed and the bridge rebuilt for traffic only.

Pont de la Tournelle, 75004

Joining the Left Bank to the Île Saint-Louis, this three-arch 24m/78.7ft stone bridge was built in 1928. It offers a wonderful view of Notre-Dame, and has a 7m/23ft-high statue of Saint Geneviève, the patron saint of Paris (by sculptor Paul Landowski, better known for his 'Christ

Pont de la Tournelle.
Ruby Boukabou

the Redeemer' statue in Rio de Janeiro, Brazil). If you can, see it at night, when it is at its moodiest.

Pont de Sully, 75005

Pont de Sully has two spans, crossing from the Right Bank, over the edge of Île Saint-Louis and over to the Left Bank near the Jean Nouvel-designed Arab World Institute. In the middle of the two spans is the lovely Square Barye (see the Bastille – Grande Mosquée walking tour) where you access a staircase leading down to the banks of the Seine, allowing you to sit and gaze under the bridge – particularly pleasant on a sunny autumn or spring morning!

Pont de Bercy.

Pont de Bercy, 75012

The Pont de Bercy is particularly eye-catching as the white and green Métro (Line 6) zips along the top of the viaducts and classic arches. There was once only a ferry here, but it became too crowded so a suspension bridge was built. The bridge was enlarged in 1906 for the Métro, then again in 1992 for more traffic, using reinforced concrete and dressed in quarry-stone facing, making it identical to the original. It's a good example of Paris' architectural layering with adjacent stairs leading down to the banks of the Seine.

Passerelle Simone-de-Beauvoir, 75012

This modern steel footbridge, named after the famous existentialist French intellectual and writer, is unique and could even been described as poetic. It curves vertically and has five points of crossing with rain shelters, connecting the Bibliothèque François-Mitterrand (Left Bank) to the Parc de Bercy (Right Bank). The design was by Paris-based Austrian architect Dietmar Feichtinger and the construction was carried out by the Eiffel Company between 2004 and 2006. The 106m x 12m prefabricated steel midsection was welded in Lauterbourg,

Passerelle Simone-de-Beauvoir. Ruby Boukabou

Alsace, and transported as a single component on barges via the Rhine, the North Sea and the Channel and installed in just one night. It is free of external support.

Bridges of Canal Saint-Martin, Canal de l'Ourcq and Canal Saint-Denis

In the thirteenth century, merchants were authorised to maintain the River Ourq and from 1517–1519, Leonardo da Vinci supposedly carried out sealed lock tests. In 1520 François I authorised merchants and alderman to make the waterways navigable in order to transport firewood and building material to Paris. Progress continued until, at the suggestion of the Prefect of Paris, Gaspard Chabrol, Napoleon ordered mathematician and engineer Pierre-Simon Girard to create the canals in 1802.

The building of the Paris canals made a huge difference to the lives of the Parisians. Water was desperately needed both for drinking and for washing the streets as cholera and dysentery were rife. Canal Saint-Denis was completed in 1821, Canal de L'Orcq in 1822 and Canal Saint-Martin in 1825.

The Parisian canal network covers 130km/80mi and today 60 per cent of Paris' unique secondary 'grey' water network for street cleaning and gardening is sourced from the canals. They are cleaned every few years and yes, the fish are saved. In 2002 an association, Au Fils de l'Ourcq, was formed for the enhancement of the natural, historical heritage of the Ourcq canal and its tributaries.

The canals feature many romantic arched cast iron footbridges, swinging bridges and locks that allow boats to pass through the various water levels. The most popular today is the Canal Saint-Martin. Lined by cafés, parks, hip clothing boutiques, wine bars and restaurants, with plenty of fresh street art splashing colour to the more classic architecture, the canals can be enjoyed by strolling along, munching or sipping by, or even cruising down on a boat.

The character Amélie (played by Audrey Tautou) skims rocks off one of the bridges in the 2001 film of the same name. Other films featuring the canals and their bridges include *Hôtel du Nord*, *Les Poupées Russes*, *Le Grand Vadrouille* and *Ocean's Twelve*, as well as clips and paintings including 'View of the Canal Saint-Martin', an 1870 painting by impressionist Alfred Sisley.

Other bridges

There are various other bridges and footbridges around Paris, even in its parks. Most have plaques with historical information. The Buttes-Chaumont footbridge is a suspension bridge designed by Gustave Eiffel, crossing high over the lake in the park. Small bridges in other parks such as Parc Monceau add both charm and practicality.

Cruises

Discover the waterways, bridges and architectural highlights of Paris while cruising the waterways. Taking a boat down the Seine and/or canal is a relaxing way to travel under the bridges, get to know their features and see how they all fit together. Most come with historic and geographical commentaries in French and English.

Canauxrama

www.canauxrama.com

Canauxrama offers several types of cruises. The two hour Saint-Martin/ Seine trip is fantastic. Book online, then meet at 71 quai de Valmy (arrive there early for a coffee at the famous Chez Prune). The boats are intimate and the friendly host talks you through the trip as you pass a swinging bridge, two locks, then descend underground and through the Bastille tunnel, out into the Arsinal Marina by Bastille, with its weeping willow tree and houseboats. You then pass under many of the bridges listed above and also spot major monuments. Mini crêpes are offered and drinks are available from the bar. A soundtrack of 'Frenchy' classics gives the final touch.

Bateaux Mouches

Port de la Conférence, 75008
www.bateaux-mouches.fr

These large double-decker boats

Ruby Bou

offer cruises up and down the Seine, allowing you to discover the bridges and monuments. You'll be sharing the voyage with a couple of hundred other tourists, which may or may not be your thing, but what's practical is their frequency (around every half hour).

Bateaux Parisiens

www.bateauxparisiens.com

Bateaux Parisiens offer both simple sightseeing trips and lunch/dinner cruises with traditional French cuisine prepared in the onboard kitchen.

Vedettes du Pont Neuf

www.vedettesdupontneuf.com

The Vedettes du Pont Neuf offer various options of cruises, including those with meals and champagne.

4

SELF-GUIDED WALKING TOURS

WHILE YOU CAN zip around Paris on the Métro, it's more rewarding to discover the city on foot. Follow these walking tours to visit iconic monuments and uncover idiosyncratic Parisian buildings and backstreets while working up an appetite to truly enjoy all those delicious French meals! Just make sure to do yourself a favour by wearing supportive shoes. For the armchair traveller – why not enjoy discovering the walks virtually via Google Earth?

WALKING TOUR 1
Paris 'Ponts' – the Central Paris Bridges

Discover the central Paris bridges by zig-zagging over and under ten of them that connect the two city islands with the right and left banks. Along the way you'll meet a bouquiniste, waft through the flower markets on the Île de la Cité, saunter along the banks of the Seine and enjoy a gelato on the Île Saint-Louis. Begin your tour around forty minutes before lunchtime to enjoy the restaurant suggestions. Flip back to the bridges chapter for more details of the

structures while crossing (see page 174).

Time: Around 2 hours, or 3-4 hours if stopping for lunch and at the attractions.

1. Pont des Arts
With your back to the grand, gilded, neo-classical Institut de France (which manages the Académie française and many foundations, museums and châteaux), cross this romantic wooden footbridge. You're likely to pass a busker, a painter and even some picnickers! At the end of the bridge turn right and head down the busy quai du Louvre until you reach ...

2. Pont Neuf
Cross the first span of the oldest bridge in Paris to arrive at the statue of Henri IV on horseback, on the Île de la Cité. Walk down the stone stairs to your right to scrutinise the bridge from beneath with its grimacing carved faces, (mascarons), designed to ward off evil spirits. Then visit the picturesque Square du Vert-Galant that literally juts out over the Seine (see page 156). Back on street

Ruby Boukabou

'My passion for books and for Paris plunges me into the heart of the city, where I can contemplate life by the Seine.' Say bonjour to Cyril and take a moment to browse his old and second-hand books, then continue to browse the other bouquinistes along quai des Grands Augustins until you arrive at Pont Saint-Michel.

Instead of crossing the bridge straight away, cross over to the right to Place Saint-Michel (see page 159) and the fountain with Saint Michael slaying the dragon, then spot Le Départ Saint-Michel bistro across the road. Stop if you need a coffee or Orangina or simply make note that this is a 24-hour bistro – handy if you have jet lag! Then cross back to the Île de la Cité via the …

level, cross over to enter the quaint Place Dauphine (see page 157). Then continue down the second span of the Pont Neuf.

Turn left onto quai des Grands Augustins and, if you're in luck, you'll find bouquiniste Cyril Graffin who says,

Walking Tour 1

Guitarist beneath Pont Saint-Michel. Ruby Boukabou

3. Pont Saint-Michel

Look up to, or visit the Sainte-Chapelle (see page 84) and Palais de Justice (see page 138), then turn right, down rue de Lutèce, passing the pretty street lamps and Cité Métro entrance before

Tour de l'Horloge, France's oldest public clock.
Ruby Boukabou

turning left to walk through the Marché aux Fleurs, a riot of colours, smells and shapes with plants, flowers and trinkets. Upon reaching the Seine, turn left and head down the quai de la Corse, looking up at the corner of the Boulevard du Palais at the Tour de l'Horloge, France's oldest public clock. If keen you can visit the Conciergerie (see page 138) or simply admire its palatial towers, before turning right to cross the...

4. Pont au Change

Imagine being back in the twelfth century and changing your currency while trying to avoid the mud splashed by passing horses and carts, then stop for a fine view of the Eiffel Tower from the far left corner. Cross over to place du Châtelet to look up to its two neo-classical theatres (see page 128), the Egyptian inspired fountain and the 1808 Roman-styled column (see page 64). With your back to the bridge, stroll right down the quai de Gesvres past more bouquinistes and be dazzled by the magnificent Hôtel de Ville (City Hall) on your left (see page 140).

Hungry? There are three great lunch options on this next stretch: Galerie 88 for delicious and affordable Mediterranean cuisine (88 quai de l'Hôtel de ville, 75004, **https:// lagalerie88.fr/**), Café Louis Philippe for Parisian bistro food and ambiance (66 quai de l'Hôtel de ville, 75004, **www. facebook.com/Cafe-Louis-Philippe**) and Chez Julien for a chic French dining experience taking you back to the 1900s (1 rue du Pont Louis-Philippe, 75004, **www.chezjulien.paris**). Then head towards the next bridge...

5. Pont Louis-Philippe
Instead of crossing the bridge, walk down to the left onto the banks of the Seine, which have been cleaned up to allow Parisians to enjoy more open, green spaces to jog, walk and relax. Stroll along past the barges (the last one before the next bridge is Péniche Marcounet, which hosts terrific jazz concerts) and check their evening programme, before climbing back up to the street to ...

6. Pont Marie
Cross the river to Île Saint-Louis, the second natural island of Paris, which prides itself on its village ambiance. You may like to explore the island and visit the Saint-Louis-en-l'Île church (19 rue Saint-Louis en l'Île, 75004), (see page 92) and enjoy a gelato at the famous Berthillon (31 rue Saint-Louis-en-l'Île). Then wrap around the quai d'Orléans and quai de Bourbon, looking over the people sitting by the Seine below (in summer, locals have picnics, play guitar, read and snooze here) until you reach...

7. Pont Saint-Louis
Cross over this short bridge back to the edge of the Île de la Cité. Chances are that there'll be a gypsy kid busking on an accordion to 'Sur le Ciel de Paris', or other musicians or street performers. On the other side of the bridge you'll find yourself behind Notre-Dame (see page 86). Then cross to the ...

8. Pont de l'Archevêché
This is the smallest bridge in Paris open to motor vehicles. On the other side, turn left and stroll down along the banks of the Seine (quai de la Tournelle) and back up to cross the ...

9. Pont de la Tournelle
Gaze up at the immense, evocative statue of Geneviève, the patron saint of Paris. Turn right to stroll down the pretty, tree-lined quai de Béthune (back on the

Saint Geneviève.
Ruby Boukabou

Quai de Béthune.
Ruby Boukabou

Île Saint-Louis) then turn right to cross back over the second span of the...

10. Pont de Sully

This is your last bridge. Hooray! Once over, cross the road and head up to the Arab World Institute to appreciate the panoramic view over Paris, including some of the bridges that you've just crossed!

WALKING TOUR 2

The Marais: Arts et Métiers to Place des Vosges

Time: Around 1.5 hours, or 4 hours if stopping at the museums and cafés.

The Marais district, spanning the 3rd and 4th arrondissements, is famous for its fashion boutiques, art galleries, hip crowds, LGBTI bars and Jewish and Chinese communities. You can spend hours exploring the narrow streets, art galleries, vintage shops and seventeenth-century private mansions. But the swampy land wasn't always so accessible. In the twelfth century there were only monks and a few sheep. It wasn't until the sixteenth and seventeenth centuries that the area was built up, with the aristocracy and nobles keen to live close to the palace (the Louvre). They often built their *hôtels particuliers* (private mansions, many of which now are now museums), behind high walls, with huge carved entrance doors in bold reds and blues. In the eighteenth century, arts and crafts workshops sprang up and while a few remain, the popularity of the area in the past few decades has seen real estate prices boom. Today there are dozens of trendy fashion boutiques, bars, cafés, art galleries and apartments.

Below is a suggested itinerary, but keep your eyes peeled as the area is full of other historical and architectural gems.

Walking Tour 2 - Part A

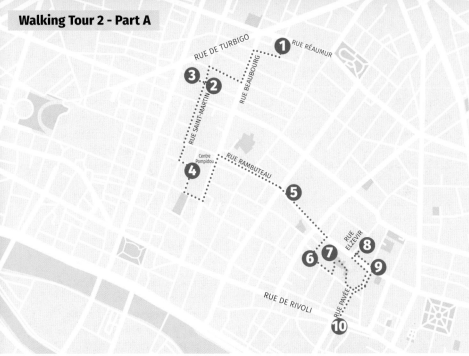

Part A: Métro Arts et Métiers to Métro Saint-Paul

If you're travelling by Métro, alight at Arts et Métiers and head down rue Réamur in the same direction as the traffic, turning right into rue Volta.

1. 3 rue Volta

Until 1979 this house with dark brown panelling on the narrow rue Volta was thought to be the oldest in Paris, dated 1240. But it turned out that it was rather a Middle Ages-styled building, constructed for a seventeenth-century Bourgeois family. It's nonetheless historic and if you can manage to find a seat at the tiny Vietnamese restaurant,

3 rue Volta. Ruby Boukabou

Song Heng, on street level, you won't regret it – their Bô Bun is delicious!

At the end of rue Volta, turn right into rue au Maire, then first left into rue Beaubourg, second right on rue Chapon, left onto rue Saint-Martin and first left again onto rue de Montmorency.

2. Maison Nicolas Flamel
51 rue de Montmorency, 75003

This building is considered the oldest stone house in Paris, dating back to 1407, where alchemist, bookseller and philanthropist Nicholas Flamel housed poor Parisians. The façade is original, with carved Latin letters requesting

Musician angel carved on the façade of the house of Nicolas Flamel. Ruby Boukabou

daily prayer from those sheltered inside. Flamel's initials are also marked in stone and the entrance is framed by four carved angels playing musical instruments – a rather nice welcoming touch! Inside, it's now an intimate, white table-clothed Michelin starred restaurant, Auberge Nicolas Flamel.

Retrace your steps back to rue Saint-Martin, cross the road, and turn down rue du Bourg l'Abbé to number 7, with its grandiose Haussmannian façade.

3. Les Bains Douches
7 rue du Bourg l'Abbe, 75003

Originally opened in 1885 by the noble family Guerbois, Les Bains was a bathhouse and massage parlour (frequented by the likes of Marcel Proust) with a restaurant for intellectuals and arty types.

When baths became more common in houses, it closed down and was in 1978 finally transformed into the nightclub 'Les Bains Douches', which became a star-studded glam/rock 'n' roll venue of the '80s (frequented by Andy Warhol, Yves Saint Laurent, Bono, Prince, David Bowie, Mick Jagger and Catherine Deneuve).

The club closed in 2010 and the establishment was taken over by French hotelier/filmmaker Jean-Pierre Marois (whose father had owned the building since the 1960s) and was reborn as a thirty-nine-room boutique hotel with restaurant, bar and nightclub (with a swimming pool!).

After checking out the bar, the artworks, the Chinese salon and the restaurant, head back to rue Saint-Martin and turn right towards...

4. Centre Pompidou

The Pompidou Centre is the pride of modern Parisian architecture, appealing to both children and adults (see page 113). Visit the top floor for a view (for a few euros), lunch at panoramic Le George restaurant, or simply do a loop of the building to consider its bold, colourful, inside-out look. If you need a coffee break, sit on the terrace of the Café Bourbourg by architect Christian de Portzamparc (43 Rue Saint-Merri), or one of the cafés by the fun Stravinsky fountain (see page 82). Or pop into the back entrance of Saint-Merri church (see page 92).

Wrap around the front of Pompidou then cross over rue Beaubourg and down Rambuteau with its boulangeries, cafés and galleries. Continue as the street becomes rue des Francs Bourgeois.

5. Musée des Archives Nationales / Hôtel de Soubise

60 rue des Francs Bourgeois, 75003

The Hôtel de Soubise was built in 1704–1709 as a private mansion for the Prince of Soubise, François de Rohan, by Pierre-Alexis Delamair and decorated by Germain Boffrand with paintings by Pierre-Charles Trémolières and his contemporaries. It's now home to the national archives and also hosts regular

Musée des Archives Nationales/Hôtel de Soubise.
Ruby Boukabou

French history exhibitions. Enter to see the show and ponder the ornate rococo interiors, or just appreciate the front garden and majestic classical style façade and arcades. As on Les Printemps department store, the statues on the building façade represent the four seasons.

NB You're also not far away from the fabulous Musée Picasso (5 rue de Thorigny, 75003) (see page 110) and Musée de la Chasse et de la Nature (60 rue des Archives, 75003) (see page 112) that are also housed in exceptional private mansions, should you like to add in visits with a small detour.

Continue down rue des Francs Bourgeois for a spot of window shopping at some of the chicest boutiques in town. Take a right into rue des Hospitalières Saint-Gervais and left into...

6. Rue des Rosiers

The heart of the Jewish quarter, this quaint cobbled street is famous for its falafel joints and high-end fashion boutiques.

7. Jardin des Rosiers - Joseph-Migneret
10 rue des Rosiers, 75004

If you've bought a falafel, find a bench in this hidden garden to munch it down as the birds serenade you. Otherwise, just stroll around it, enjoying the calmness and the scent of rosemary from the herb gardens behind the large houses.

Continue down rue des Rosiers, turn left onto rue Pavée, left back onto rue des Francs Bourgeois and then right into rue Elzevir.

8. Musée Cognacq-Jay
8 rue Elzevir, 75003

An early example of the *hôtel particulier*, this private mansion dates back to the late sixteenth century. It was home to the royal surveyor Médéric de Donon and now houses the private collection of Ernest Cognacq and Marie-Louise Jay, founders of the Samaritaine department store (see page 57).

Retrace your steps back down Elzevir and turn left onto rue des Francs Bourgeois.

9. Musée Carnavalet
17 rue des Francs Bourgeois, 75003

The Musée Carnavalet celebrates the history of Paris. Inside you can discover many buildings that no longer stand today. The building was constructed in 1548, renovated in the seventeenth century by François Mansart and opened as a museum in 1880. It has undergone several

Paris Tourist Office, Amélie Dupont

make-overs over the years (see page 112).

Cross the road and head back down rue Pavée until you hit rue de Rivoli. If you're beat you can leave here via Saint-Paul Métro, but Part B is only half an hour, so why not just take a coffee/meal break at...

10. La Favorite
6 rue de Rivoli, 75004
(**www.lafavorite-paris.com**)

This vintage-styled Paris meets New York brasserie/bistro is just lovely, with its black and white tiled floors, wooden tables and chairs and hanging ceiling fans, lighting and heating. Best of all, the menu ranges from croque monsieurs to BLTs!

Part B: Métro Saint-Paul to Place des Vosges

1. Métro Saint-Paul

From Métro Saint-Paul, head down rue du Prévôt, turning right into rue Charlemagne and an immediate left into rue du Figuier – the sweet scent of the fig trees will give a spring to your step. The first fig tree was said to be planted here in the seventeenth century by Marguerite de Valois, a former resident of...

2. Hôtel de Sens

At the end of the street you'll find what looks like a castle from a fairy tale, with its pointed turrets and French gardens.

Hôtel de Sens. Ruby Boukabou

The building was constructed in 1519 for the bishops of Sens, but now houses the Forney art library and has a lovely French garden behind it.

Wrap around the building and head left up rue Fauconnier, passing the MIJE youth hostel, housed in a large seventeenth-century building covered

Walking Tour 2 - Part B

dramatically in vines.

Turn right down rue Charlemagne (if you need a coffee or meal, the traditional French restaurant Chez Mademoiselle on the corner at number 16 is cosy and friendly).

3. Old Wall of Paris

Stroll down the narrow rue Charlemagne with its coloured street posts and you'll arrive at the relics of the old wall of Paris, on the rue des Jardins Saint-Paul, constructed on the orders of Philippe-Auguste from 1190 to 1215 to protect the city from invasion.

To the right is a sports field and to the left, under the black silhouette of Saint-Paul-Saint-Louis church is the...

4. Fontaine du Lycée Charlemagne

Built in 1840, this stone fountain features the coat of arms of Paris and a cast iron basin carried by dolphins and decorated with the statue of a smiling young boy, carrying a shell.

Turn left onto rue Saint-Paul and step into the tiny cul-de-sac rue Eginhard and you'll spy an old stone wall fountain, 'Fountain Eginhard', although it's no longer functional. Continue along Rue Saint-Paul.

Fontaine du Lycée Charlemagne. Ruby Boukabou

Twelfth century wall of Paris.
Ruby Boukabou

5. Église Saint-Paul-Saint-Louis

Pop into the Saint-Paul-Saint-Louis church, built under Louis XIII in the mid-seventeenth century (see page 91). Light a candle, say a prayer or just take a moment to sit and look up to the beautiful dome ceiling above the choir.

Cross rue Saint-Antoine and head right (against the traffic). On your left at number 48 is …

6. Hôtel de Sully

48 rue Sainte-Antoine, 75004
www.hotel-de-sully.fr/en

While the building, now housing the seat

Église Saint-Paul-Saint-Louis. Ruby Boukabou

of the Centre of National Monuments, is not open to visitors, it does have a lovely bookshop. Walk through and out to the pretty and aromatic French garden. Look back to admire the seventeenth-century private mansion commissioned by Henry IV (likely by architect Jean Androuet du Cerceau) and shortly after bought by the incorruptible Duke of Sully, who added an extra wing. It stayed in the Sully family until the mid-eighteenth century and guests included Madame de Sévigné (the marquise de Sévigné, known for her fine, witty letters) and Voltaire.

Float through the gardens and you'll find a discrete entrance to...

7. Place des Vosges

Once called the Place Royale, this royal commission by the public spirited and forward-thinking King Henri IV was Paris' first planned square (see page 158). It was a multi-purpose space to accommodate housing, industry and retail. Enjoy the Renaissance feel for order, symmetry and geometry with the identical surrounding and connected apartments with French windows above covered arcades.

Visit Victor Hugo's apartment (which he rented from 1832 to 1848), now a small museum dedicated to the writer (see page 114). Finally, find a bench in the grassy square to rest your legs!

WALKING TOUR 3
Bastille to La Grande Mosquée de Paris

This tour weaves back and forth through the ages. You'll begin on the pivotal site of the French Revolution, travel down to the banks of the Seine, cross over historic bridges, under the statue of the patron saint of Paris (Saint Geneviève), climb the contemporary Institut du Monde Arabe (see page 114), wander through the riverside sculpture gardens and the botanical gardens, and finish in the teahouse of the beautiful neo-byzantine mosque (see page 106).

Time: 1 hour or 3-4 hours if stopping at the attractions.

1. Opéra Bastille (see page 127)

Alight at Bastille Métro and take the Opéra exit. Look up the grand staircase to the contemporary curved design of the Bastille Opera house by Uruguayan architect Carlos Ott – a complete contrast to the ornate Palais Garnier. Boring and ugly or slick and smooth? You decide.

Absorb the buzz of Bastille with its large terrace cafés and huge central roundabout with traffic flying in all directions, and remember that this was the area where the Bastille prison stood (and was stormed during the 1789 French Revolution).

Cross to the middle of the roundabout.

Walking Tour 3

Ruby Boukabou

at number 18. Continue to boulevard Morland to find the...

3. Pavillon de l'Arsenal
21 boulevard Morland, 75004
(**www.pavillon-arsenal.com**)

This centre of architecture and urban planning is the point of reference for the serious architecture lovers among you! Around the walls you can see and read the history of Paris architecture from the Middle Ages and into the future, with pictures and descriptions in French and English. This 'Paris, a city in the making' timeline contains over 1,000 archived documents, photographs, maps, plans and films. They have done a terrific job and you could literally take days to read it and take it all in. There's a good little bookshop on the ground floor and a research room upstairs (open on Tuesdays and Thursdays 1pm–6pm).

Return to boulevard Henri IV and head left towards the...

2. Colonne de Juillet (see page 65)
With its bronze winged 'genie of freedom' glinting on top, the July Column is a memorial to the 1830 Revolution and is even more arresting when standing directly underneath it.

On the left is the Bassin de l'Arsenal, where the canal Saint-Martin emerges from its underground passage and joins the Seine.

Cross boulevard Bourdon and take boulevard Henri IV, passing by the grand, stone national Police headquarters

Pavillon de l'Arsenal. Ruby Boukabou

4. Pont de Sully
Cross the first stretch of the bridge then duck left into the...

5. Square Barye
Walk through this lovely little park and down the stone stairs to the right. Sit on the bank of the Seine and gaze under the second stretch of the Pont de Sully and the Pont de la Tournelle (see page 179).

Head back towards the second stretch of Pont de Sully. If you've already done the bridges tour you may want to cross straight over the second stretch and left into the Tino-Rossi Gardens, otherwise ... stroll right down the romantic, tree-lined quai de Béthune, and turn left to cross the...

View of Pont Sully and the Arab World Institute.
Ruby Boukabou

6. Pont de la Tournelle (see page 179)
Cross to the other side for a good view of the back of Notre-Dame. Then cross back over to say bonjour to Geneviève, the patron saint of Paris, whose statue looms high overhead.

Head back towards Pont de Sully and cross the quai de La Tournelle.

7. Arab World Institute (see page 114)
Be dazzled by Jean Nouvel's contemporary masterpiece: an aluminium and glass complex that promotes conversations between the Arab world and Western culture. Their exhibitions are fantastic but if you don't have time, just head to the top floor for a panoramic view over Paris, and in particular, the Île de la Cité. On the way out, visit their ground-floor bookshop. Most books are in Arabic or French,

View from the Arab World Institute. Ruby Boukabou

but there are adorable notebooks with geometrical Arabic motifs that may inspire you to write or jot notes about your explorations and observations.

Cross back over quai Saint-Bernard to...

8. Tino-Rossi Garden
Along this stretch of the Seine is an open-air sculpture gallery with the works of Brâncuşi, César, Zadkine and many others between a willow tree, green areas and small amphitheatres (where you can tango and salsa dance on summer nights).

Cross back over the quai de La Tournelle.

9. Jardin des Plantes (see page 150)
Enter the botanical gardens, stroll down tree-lined passages, marvel at old plants (the pistachio tree is over 300 years old)

and discover the greenhouses and the neo-classical Mineralogy and Geology Gallery (Charles Rohault de Fleury, 1836). Stand and be amazed under the massive seventeenth-century National Museum of Natural History by Jules André with its nineteenth-century stone façade.

Jardin des Plantes. Ruby Boukabou

Tip – if you're peckish and not planning to have lunch at the restaurant at the mosque, grab a cheap, delicious wrap or mahejab (savoury Algerian crêpe) from Le Jardin de Jazmin, 75 rue Buffon, 75005, and come back and eat it in the garden.

Exit the park at the top left corner and cross Rue Geoffroy-Saint-Hilaire

10. Grande Mosquée de Paris (see page 106)
2bis Place du Puits de l'Ermite, 75005

Time to reward yourself with a sweet mint tea and baklava under an olive tree at a mosaic table in the courtyard teahouse at the back of the grand mosque. There is also a beautiful and cosy Algerian restaurant with continual service from lunch to dinner. Once you're done with couscous or tea, walk around to the front of the mosque to gaze up at the intricate, beautiful minaret and visit the interior. Or ladies, it's time to head into the hammam (Turkish baths). *Saha!*

NB it's just a 10 minute stroll to Walk 4, however, you will likely appreciate it more when fresh another day. The closest Métro is Jussieu.

Grande Mosquée de Paris. Ruby Boukabou

WALKING TOUR 4

Arènes de Lutèce to Église Saint-Julien-le-Pauvre

This tour is bookended with relics of Roman Paris (Lutetia or Lutèce in French), starting at the ancient arena and finishing just after the Cluny Museum with its ancient Roman baths. In between you'll discover more of the twelfth century wall around Paris, climb the hill of Geneviève – the cradle of Paris (with its Saint-Étienne-du-Mont church and the mighty Pantheon mausoleum) – get pensive by the Sorbonne and royally relaxed in the Luxembourg gardens.

Time: 2 hours, or around 4 hours if you visit the attractions.

Arènes de Lutèce. Ruby Boukabou

Ruby Boukabou

Part A: Arènes de Lutèce to Luxembourg Gardens

1. Arènes de Lutèce

Close by Métro Jussieu or Cardinal Lemoine, this arena is one of the few remaining relics of Roman Lutetia. Perch up above and imagine watching a Roman play or a gladiator fight. If you're in luck, your imagination may be stimulated by some live action of young men practising their fencing (and you'll probably see some old men playing petanque!).

Turn right up rue Monge, first left onto rue du Cardinal Lemoine and second right onto rue Clovis.

2. Twelfth-century wall of Paris

On your left you'll pass another part of the ancient Paris wall that you saw in the Marais walk. In 1190, before leaving for his crusade, Philippe-Auguste asked the citizens to help construct a stone wall around Paris. It was completed in 1215 and what remains here was formerly part of a tower.

Continue uphill.

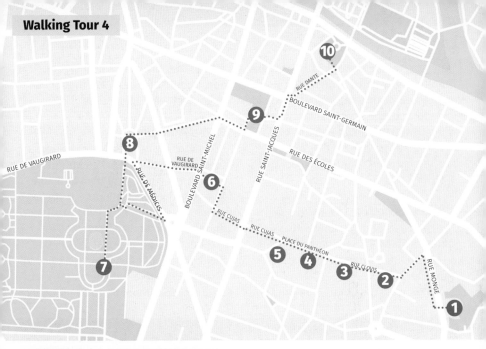

3. Saint-Étienne-du-Mont
Place Sainte-Geneviève, 75005
This magnificent fifteenth-century
church (see page 93) sits on the hill
Sainte-Geneviève, the cradle of Paris.

Ruby Boukabou

Your gaze will be drawn in all directions, from the large balcony organ to the golden ceiling decorations. Back outside, look down to the stairs – these were where Owen Wilson's character sat before going back in time in Woody Allen's charming feature film *Midnight in Paris*.

4. Sainte-Geneviève Library (see page 142)
Pass by this stately buildng with students lining up and tourists resting on the creative stone street seating opposite.

Just beyond the library, you will spot part of the Sorbonne – fittingly classical and grand (12 Place du Panthéon) –but to your left and unmissable is...

5. The Panthéon
No matter if you've been here several times before or never, the enormity and neo-classical design of the Pantheon (see page 165) is astounding. If you're travelling with someone who proclaims that they aren't much interested in architecture, this is the place to take them. It's impossible not to feel moved when staring up at the mammoth columns, Corinthian portico and temple-

Inside the Panthéon.
Ruby Boukabou

Ruby Boukabou

like dome. Enter to be mesmerised by a replica of Faucoult's 1851 pendulum, frescoes, mosaics and paintings, then wind down the stairs to the crypt to pay your respects to Victor Hugo, Émile Zola, Voltaire and Marie Curie (the first woman to join the 'great men' of France) among others. Between April and October you can access the colonnade of the dome for a bird's eye view over the Latin Quarter and Paris.

Head down rue Cujas on the right with the Pantheon behind you and turn right when you reach rue Victor Cousin until you reach …

6. Place de La Sorbonne

Stand in the Sorbonne square (see pages 141 & 159) and try to catch the passing ideas in the air from the thirteenth century until today. Consider this quote from André Malraux, France's first Cultural Affairs Minister under President de Gaulle, which is displayed on a plaque at le Tour Zamansky in the Jussieu campus (located 10 mins away, near the Arab World Institute): 'The future is a present given to us by the past.'

Walk through the square, passing the fountains and cafés, and cross over boulevard Saint-Michel then continue down rue Vaugirard until you hit the Luxembourg Gardens. Just to the left before crossing to the gardens, at 5 rue de Médicis, the Treize au Jardin Café (http://treizeaujardin.com) is a great, cosy, bilingual café for fresh juices, pots of tea and delicious cakes and meals. Right next door is English bookshop The Red Wheelbarrow. Say hi to owner Penelope and pick up White Owl sister publications to this book of The Food Lover's Guide to Paris (by Helen Massey-Beresford) and my The Art Lover's Guide to Paris, and/or a ripping yarn set in Paris.

7. Jardin du Luxembourg (see page 151)

Explore these superb public gardens. The Louis XIII-style Palais de Luxembourg now houses the senate and is not open to the public, but you can certainly admire it while sitting by the lake and strolling through the gardens with its sculptures, flower beds, tennis courts, bandstand and playgrounds. If you love a good hot chocolate, head to Angelina – a sister of the famous rue de Rivoli tearoom, in the Musée de Luxembourg (see page 115).

If you're tired (especially if you've continued from the previous tour), you can finish the tour here with an exhibition, or by lounging on the grass in the gardens. You're right next to Luxembourg train station that connects to transport both within and outside central Paris. Or to continue…

Part B: Luxembourg Gardens – Saint-Julien-Le-Pauvre

After enjoying one of the prettiest gardens in Paris, take one of the north exits and head off down rue Rotrou, following along the side wall of the

Odeon Theatre to arrive at the ...

8. Place de l'Odeon/Odeon Théâtre

This semi-circular 'place' has the theatre as its main attraction. (See page 129)

Facing the theatre, take the street on your left, rue Racine, to its end and cross boulevard Saint-Michel into rue des Écoles. On the left you'll find ...

9. Musée de Cluny

This Middle Ages Museum, with the famous 'Lady and the Unicorn' tapestries, also boasts the vestiges of Gallo-Roman baths. (See page 115)

Head out and left down rue Saint-Jacques, right onto rue Galande and left again into rue Saint-Julien le Pauvre.

Ruby Boukabou

10. Saint-Julien-le-Pauvre

79 rue Galande, 75005
Enjoy a quiet moment of reflection in one of Paris' oldest religious buildings. (See page 93)

WALKING TOUR 5

Covered Passages ('Galleries') – Palais-Royal to Passage Verdeau

Time warps exist in Paris in the form of covered passages ('galeries') – glass-roofed arcades with ornate decorations. Inside? Charming boutiques of stamp and postcard collectors, antique canes, décor and toys as well as cute restaurants and teahouses.

These city arcades were mostly built in the nineteenth century, with a boom in 1850s, and are principally located on the Right Bank in central Paris. They provided pleasant ways in which pedestrians could travel between streets, protected by the elements, particularly when they became lit and heated by gas. They offered plenty of occasions for '*flâneurs*' – at least the sort with money as there were no benches or places to loiter, but rather cafés, boutiques and paid reading rooms to spend time and cash.

While 150 or so were originally constructed, their patronage declined after the large department stores took over and Haussmann redesigned the city and cleaned up the streets. There are around three dozen that remain, each

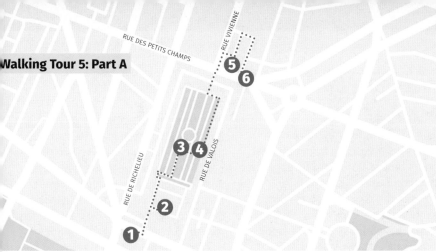

with its own personality: from theatrical (there is literally a theatre off the Passage des Panoramas and a wax museum

Tour guide Alissia Bedr. Ruby Boukabou

off Passage Jouffroy) to treasure trove (Passage Verdeau for antique shops) and Indian (Passage Brady in the 10th is part of Little India). Most are open 8am–8pm, some are closed on Sundays.

Follow this suggested itinerary or contact passionate tour guide Alissia Bedr (alissia.bedr@gmail.com, @ alissiabinparis) for a personalised tour here or for various other tours.

*Time: 2 hours in order to discover these five covered passages at a leisurely pace. Start half an hour before lunch and add an hour or two if you want to enjoy the iconic brasserie Le Grand Colbert (**https://legrandcolbert.fr**)!*

Part A: Palais-Royal to Galerie Vivienne

1. Place Colette

If you're arriving by Métro, alight at Palais Royal (lines 1 and 7) and take exit 5 to Place Colette, itself a colourful contemporary art work called the 'Kiosque des noctambules'.

Walk towards the Comédie-Française (see page 129) and into the courtyard of...

2. Palais-Royal

Louis XIV lived here briefly as a child and a late-night escape from potential revolters proved traumatising, possibly one of the reasons why he felt safer later in life residing outside of Paris, in Versailles (see page 167).

It was the infamous Louis-Philippe (king of France 1830-1848) who commercialised the residence by opening a shopping and entertainment complex. The streets of Paris were filthy but here people would pass by an entrance with shoe cleaning tools and services to remove the mud from their boots before they entered to shop, window-shop and, above all, socialise. Since the property was officially private, the police didn't interfere and things became quite debauched at night with gambling and prostitution.

Today, the black and white striped columns of Daniel Buren add a playfulness to the square. Made of white and black Pyrenees marble, as used by artists such as Michelangelo and Rodin, and set in straight lines at even spaces, they maintain a uniformity despite their different heights. Like many installations, they were both loved and hated by the public on construction in 1985.

3. Jardin du Palais-Royal

To the left is a lovely rose garden where locals can escape the buzz of the traffic and the wind with a good book on a sunny day... (see page 150)

4. Palais-Royal Galleries

Stroll through these galleries with their high-end boutiques, above which you'll notice the arched windows that were once the rooms for the higher class of prostitutes, the 'coquettes'. Floor mosaics, columns and rustic lamps now give the arcades a sense of grandeur.

Out the other side of the arcade, turn left onto rue Beaujolais and look up to see Colette's residence (number 9), marked with a plaque, where the writer lived from 1927–1929, then from 1932 until her death in 1954. Turn immediately right up rue Vivienne.

5. Galerie Colbert

4 rue Vivienne, 75002
Galerie Colbert was built in 1823 as a rival to Galerie Vivienne. However, it never reached the same success and fell into abandonment. The passage was saved from destruction in the 1980s by the national library and doesn't house boutiques but instead the Institut Nationale d'Histoire de l'Art (INHA) and the Institut National du Patrimoine (heritage). The architectural highlight is its rotunda topped with a glass dome underneath – a statue of Eurydice being bitten by a snake. Wander through the classical themed gallery with faux beams and a portrait painting of Colbert (Minister of Finances 1661–1683 under Louis XIV) and

Le Grand Colbert.

glance into university lectures taking place. At the other end you can enter the famous Art Nouveau brasserie 'Le Grand Colbert', which features in many French and international films. If you plan on having lunch here, book in advance and set aside a few hours – it's the sort of place you'll want to drink in the ambiance without being rushed over your crème brûlée!

You'll come out onto rue des Petits Champs. Head left, against the traffic, and turn briefly left onto rue des Petits Pères, then left again onto rue de la Banque.

6. Galerie Vivienne
5 rue de la Banque, 75002
One of the most adored covered passages in Paris today is Galerie Vivienne, also built in 1823. The colourful mosaic floors with stars and swirls were created by Italian mosaic artist Giandomenico Facchina (who also decorated Charles Garnier's Palais Garnier opera house and restored ancient mosaics in St Mark's Basilica, Venice). Giandomenico employed a groundbreaking technique of placing the pieces together on sheets in his workshop to save time on site.

Galerie Vivienne.

RUE DE LA GRANGE BATELIÉRE ③

BOULEVARD HAUSSMANN ②

RUE VIVIENNE ①

Part B: Passage des Panoramas to Passage Verdeau

1. Passage des Panoramas

11 boulevard Montmartre, 75002

The Passage des Panoramas was an early procurer to 3D if you will – an attraction from American inventor Robert Fulton – two rotundas displayed panoramic paintings of Paris, Toulon, Rome and other large cities. Fulton financed himself with this invention while awaiting Napoleon's response to his proposed submarine and other inventions, then left for London when he declined.

From 1816 gas lighting illuminated the passage, full of craftsmen stores and eateries. The wooden ceiling was replaced by iron and glass, but some of the existing façades remain as historic monuments – including the intricate wooden framing of the Chocolatier Marquis (now a restaurant) and the sign for Stern printing house. Postcard and

The high glass roof allows in natural light and the decorations reference Greek antiquity, such as carved wings and the helmet of Mercury, the god of commerce. Boutiques include a cellar and wine bar, restaurants and, most famously, Jousseaume bookshop (45-47), which opened in 1826 and has stayed in the same family ever since. Regulars included the author Colette. It doubled as a reading room where people would pay per hour or half a day to browse books and papers or, it's said, to exchange secretive information...

Turn right out of the galley and head down rue Vivienne, across rue du 4 Septembre, right into rue Feydeau, left down rue des Panoramas, right onto rue Saint-Marc and left into ...

Passage des Panoramas.
Ruby Boukabou

stamp collectors could spend hours in this passageway alone. The 1807 inaugurated Théâtre des Variétés' artist entrance is through the passage.

Cross the boulevard Montmartre to...

2. Passage Jouffroy
10-12 boulevard Montmartre, 75009
Passage Jouffroy and the following passage Verdeau were the combined works of architects of the same names.

Passage Jouffrey was the first to open, in 1836. It featured a double glass ceiling with a pointed arch, marble pavings, and introduced the first underground heating (women could stand over the grates for some hot air up their dresses in winter). The neighbouring wax museum Musée Grévin is here and visitors leave via the passage, which helped maintain its popularity over the years. There's a walking stick store, a toy store, a delightful Christmassy trinket boutique, a photography shop, antique bookshops and a tearoom called Valentin. If you check-in to Hotel Chopin, make sure to ask for room 409, which has a view over the passageway.

Cross over the rue de la Grange Batelière to…

3. Passage Verdeau
6 rue de la Grange-Batelière, 75003
With a fishbone-style high glass roof and charming shops of cameras, postcards and old books, this is a lovely little passage to finish your stroll, or to take a break before heading off to discover more. Have a drink at 'Le Bistro' with its red benches, wooden chairs, ceiling beams and resident black cat. Perhaps it's a good time to go old fashioned and handwrite some vintage postcards?

Other passages to explore while you're on a roll:

Passage du Grand-Cerf
145 rue Saint-Denis, 75002
Made of metal and wrought iron with 12m/39ft-high glass ceilings, this pretty

arcade was opened in 1825 and houses cafés and boutiques of jewellery, clothing, furniture and antiques.

Passage des Princes
5 boulevard des Italiens, 75002
The current passage des Princes is actually a 1995 recreation of the original (1860–1985). The coloured glass domes, however, date back to the 1930s. It's now overtaken with game shops, from video games to toys to Harry Potter pop-ups.

Passage Choiseul
40 rue des Petits Champs, 75002
Restored and reopened in 2013, the glass roof can be admired here over a Bio Burger or even a siesta, massage or fish foot spa at Bar à Sieste!

Passage du Caire
2 place du Caire, 75002
The oldest standing and longest arcade in Paris is the 370m/1214ft-long Passage du Caire, which opened in 1798 as a centre for printers and lithographers. Egyptian Revival decorations abound including Egyptian cow-headed goddess Hathor statues welcoming pedestrians and lotus and papyrus leaves upon columns. Overhead is a fishbone-styled glass roof (originally wooden). Check out the heritage façades of the upper floors as you pass by the (mostly wholesale) clothing boutiques.

Galerie de la Madeleine
9 place de la Madeleine, 75008
Smart and elegant, this passage, constructed in the 1840s by architect

Théodore Charpentier, leads to the Madeleine church (see page 99). It is well preserved and today houses luxury boutiques and cafés and features two caryatides in the main entrance.

Galerie Véro-Dodat

19 rue de Jean-Jacques Rousseau, 75001
Close by the Louvre, the Galerie Véro-Dodat is short but chic, with diamond-shaped marble pavings, glass, and engraved ceilings. Here you'll find the Christian Louboutin workshop-boutique, antique dolls and art galleries.

WALKING TOUR 6
Theatrical Paris: Gare Saint-Lazare to Place Vendôme

There are hundreds of iconic performance venues in Paris, such as the Opéra Garnier, opulent theatres such as Théâtre de l'Athénée, and legendary music halls including the Olympia. But the city of Paris is theatrical in itself. The major train stations and boulevards are grand, the department stores dramatic and the hotels often palatial. This tour passes by all of the above, beginning at the Gare Saint-Lazare, passing by Opéra Garnier and finishing at the Ritz.

1. Gare Saint-Lazare

Alight from the Métro at Saint-Lazare (see page 60), coming out at the 2012 renovated passenger hall with its spick glass and wooden three-level shopping

Walking Tour 6

RUE SAINT-LAZARE
RUE DU HAVRE
RUE DE PROVENCE
BOULEVARD HAUSSMANN
RUE AUBER
RUE SCRIBE
RUE DE CAUMARTIN
BOULEVARD DES CAPUCINES
RUE DES CAPUCINES
RUE DE LA PAIX
PLACE VENDÔME

complex that sits under the original ceilings with natural skylights. Exit to the front of the station, taking a moment to look up at the classically inspired façade. If you're panicked about timing, let yourself be relieved by French artist Arman's 1985 sculpture *L'heure de tous*: a tower of dozens of bronze clock faces stuck together, all reading different times.

Cross the road and head straight down rue Intérieure in the same direction as the traffic, turn left onto rue Saint-Lazare, immediately right onto rue du Harve then first left onto rue de Provence. Look up!

2. Printemps Haussmann

Admire the façade of the 'cathedral of commerce', a stone-clad, iron-framed structure with its magnificent Art Deco cupola (see page 54). Enter Printemps Homme (Men's Department) and head to the ninth floor. Gasp at the panorama over the capital. The rooftop restaurant is cosy and panoramic (and the Perruche

Printemps Haussmann. Ruby Boukabou

cocktail bar during summer is here). Then head back down and out then back into the adjacent Women's Department. On the sixth floor is the Art Deco 'Brasserie Printemps' (redesigned by Didier Gomez) sitting under a magical kaleidoscope of a 1923-built canopy. Even if you're not stopping to eat or drink, it's a stunning site to behold.

Continue down boulevard Haussmann to...

3. Galeries Lafayette (see page 55)

Printemps isn't the only one to showcase a beautiful canopy. At Galeries Lafayette, the stained-glass domed ceiling is the central attraction with the operatic gilded balconies. Avoid being sucked into a shopping spree and instead head to the seventh-floor rooftop of the main store via the escalators for another panoramic view – this time just over the back of Opéra Garnier. In winter there's even a mini ice-skating rink for kids.

Time to visit Garnier's architectural masterpiece! For a visit enter through the arch opposite the Galereis Lafayette,

Galeries Lafayette. Ruby Boukabou

at the side of the building on rue Scribe. Afterwards walk around to study the building's brilliant front façade.

4. Palais Garnier (see page 126)

Give yourself around half-an-hour inside the Palais Garnier opera house (tour tickets available from machines at the entrance), climbing up the magnificent marble staircase, peering at the ceiling painted by Chagall in the splendid red and golden main auditorium, and floating around the galleries fit for an emperor. It's like a slice of Versailles in Paris. Even if you don't enter, the front of the building is a vision in itself, with its ornate lamps, the personified gilded 'Harmony' and 'Poetry' by Charles Gumery, the busts of composers (Rossini, Beethoven, Mozart...) and sculptured, gilded interpretations of Lyrical Drama and Lyrical Poetry.

Ruby Boukabou

Turn right into rue Auber (when your back is to the opera, heading in the opposite direction to the traffic), take the first left into rue Boudreau, then left again into...

5. Square de l'Opéra Louis-Jouvet & Théâtre de l'Athénée

This small, peaceful square is a pleasant contrast to the buzz of the boulevards. Named after French actor Louis Jouvet (1887–1951), the director of the 1896 inaugurated Italian-styled Théâtre de l'Athénée, the building has a flamboyant Art Nouveau façade. In the centre of the square is a bronze statue of a mythical winged horse about to take off into a dream-world, sculpted by Alexandre Falguière in 1897. If you're ready for lunch, Paparazzi (https://paparazzi-paris.fr/en) at number 6, is an elegant Italian restaurant.

Continue through the square to arrive at ...

6. Place Edward VII

At the centre of the square is a statue of Paris lover, the British King Edward VII on horseback.

Orson Welles was one of the many anglophone actors and directors who performed at the Théâtre Edouard VII here. Pop in for the programme (see page 130) then continue through the square, swinging right through the rather royal looking gateway to do a loop (of the courtyard). The geometric shapes on the buildings of Felice Varini play an optical illusion as they travel between buildings to create their forms.

Back in Place Edward VII, turn left down rue Bruno Coqatrix and take the first left onto rue de Caumartin. Step into number 6 on the left.

7. Le Petit Olympia
6 rue de Caumartin, 75009
www.lepetitolympia.com

Originally the Bar Romain, this Roman themed bar/restaurant is associated with many stars and their entourage who have spent time before or after their concert at the adjoining Olympia music hall. Elegant and theatrical with comforting woodwork and a large mirror making the space seem larger, the intimate café is decorated with chandeliers, paintings of Ancient Rome, columns and photo walls of the stars that have passed through, and of the Olympia bill for shows such as Louis Armstrong and his orchestra.

Continue down rue de Caumartin and cross the boulevard des Capucines to look back at ...

8. L'Olympia (see page 132)
28 boulevard des Capucines, 75009

This mythic music hall (opened by the original owners of the Moulin Rouge) has played host to the likes of Edith Piaf, Charles Aznavour, Dalida, The Beatles and many more. Checking the programme for the evening is easy – the billing is the main feature of the façade.

With your back to l'Olympia walk straight down rue des Capucines (not boulevard des Capucines). At Place Vendôme turn right.

9. Place Vendôme (see page 66)

Built under Louix XIV, this square certainly feels exceptionally royal and epic, with its classical urban design, elegant Hausmannian buildings, stone pavements and a central victory column. Cross to the centre and study the surface of the bronze column made from 1,200 enemy canons topped by a statue of Napoleon Bonaparte.

Time to relax in style. Cross over to number 15.

10. The Ritz (see page 44)
15 Place Vendôme, 75001

The Ritz hotel opened in 1898. After a four-year $400 million renovation, finished in 2016, it is now the height of luxury more than ever, with beautiful Belle Époque décor. Treat yourself to an infusion in the library bar or inner courtyard café, or if it's after 6pm there's the famous Bar Hemingway for some old world charm and a Serendipity (calvados from Le Pays d'Auge and apple juice with bitter apples from Normandy, fresh mint, and Champagne) created (and usually served) by their legendary head barman Colin Field. *Santé!*

Paris Architecture in Painting

I hope you've had a fabulous time in, on and around the buildings of Paris! Want to take something special home? Why not treat yourself or a loved one to an artist's interpretation of the architecture of Paris? Visit 59 Rivoli Artist Studios (59 rue de Rivoli, 75001), or Place de Tertre in Montmartre and you'll also find many other galleries and studios in my book' *The Art Lover's Guide to Paris.*

Here are three artists you may especially like. Contact them via their websites for appointments. You'll also often find James and David at 59 Rivoli. Ask for them at the entrance.

David Twose
www.davidtwose.com

Linda McClusky
www.lindamccluskey.com

James Purpura
www.jamespurple.com

BIBLIOGRAPHY

Ayres, Andrew, *The Architecture of Paris, an Architectural Guide*, Edition Axel Menges, Stuttgart, 2004

Clausen, Meredith L., 06/2010 The Ecole des Beaux-Arts: Toward a Gendered History, 01/06/2010, Journal of the Society of Architectural Historians (2010), Volume 69, Issue 2

Collard, Susan, 'The Architecture of Power: Francois Mitterrand's *Grand Travaux* Revisited', in *International Journal of Cultural Policy* 14: 2, pp.195 – 208, SEI, University of Sussex, 2008

Coulin, G., *Lutecia, the Gallo-Roman Ancestor of Paris*, Medico Graphia Vol 34. No. 2, 2012

Darke, Diana, *Stealing from the Saracens: How Islamic Architecture Shaped Europe*, Hurst Publishers, London, 2020

DK Eyewitness Paris: 2019, D K Publishing, Penguin Random House, London, 2018

Earle, Dominic (ed.), *Time Out*, Time Out Digital Limited, London, 2015

Heran, Emmanuelle, *The Tuileries Garden, Yesterday and Today: A Walker's Guide*, Musée de Louvre Publication Service, 2016

Horn Christian, Basile Maria, De Laelu, Thibaut, Vialan Daphne, La défense 2050, *International Workshop of Urban Planning & Design 2011*, ateliers.org/en 2011

Maclean M. (ed.) *The Mitterrand Years, Legacy and Evaluation*: Palgrave Macmillan, London. https://doi.org/10.1007/978-1-349-26395-0_16, 1998

Reisenberger Ruth, Sienkowska Lucy, Walker Penny, *Paris 2019*, D K Publishing, Penguin Random House, 2018

Scicolone, Maria, *Developing Skyscraper districts: La Défense*, CTBUH Journal 2012, Issue 1

Shapiro, Ann-Louise, *Housing the Poor of Paris, 1850–1902*, University of Wisconsin Press, 1985

Stott, Carolyn, *Belleville rouge, Belleville noir, Belleville rose: The complex identity of a Parisian quartier*, (https://creativecommons.org/licenses/by/4.0/) PORTAL Journal of Multidisciplinary International Studies, vol.12, no. 1, January 2015

Texter, Simon, *Paris Panorama de l'architecture de l'Antiquite a nos jours*, Parigramme 2012

Tschumi Bernard, Derrida Jacques,

Van Uffelen Chris, Gosler Markus, Paris the Architecture Guide, 2009

Vidler Anthony, *Parc de la Villette*, Artifice, 2014

White, Norval, *The Guide to the Architecture of Paris*, Charles Scribner's Sons, Macmillan Publishing Company, New York 1991

Websites include:

www.britannica.com

www.catacombes.paris.fr/en

www.france24.com

www.gouvernement.fr

www.metro.paris.en

www.parisfutur.com

www.planete-energies.com/en

www.historyfiles.co.uk

www.newgeography.com

https://www.theartstory.org/

INDEX

Materials (Building & Decorative)